SAP Sales and Distribution Quick Configuration Guide

Advanced SAP Tips and Tricks with Variant Configuration

SYED AWAIS RIZVI

ITSAS LLC PUBLICATIONS

Author: **Syed Awais Rizvi**

Executive Project Manager: Syed Imon Rizvi and Syed Ali Qasim

Technical Editor: Raza Naqvi, Alizer Rizvi

Graphical Development and Editor: Imtayaz Abbas

Production Manager: Syed Riyaz Hussain

Project Coordinator: Syed Raza Naqvi

ISBN: 1942554060
ISBN: 978-1-942554-06-6

Library of Congress Control Number: 015905475

Publishers ITSAS LLC | ITSAS.US | Anaheim California

DEDICATION

Start with name of God, most gracious and most merciful.

God! Send your blessings to our Prophet Muhammad (peace be upon him) and his Ahl al-Bayt.

Thanks to my dear Mother and Father.

Special thanks to my dear wife Sairah for all the support and understanding.

Thanks to my family and friends for all the support and inspiration.

There is no greater wealth than wisdom, no greater poverty than ignorance, no greater heritage than culture, and no greater support than consultation.

Imam Ali (A.S) Nahgulbalagah

50 Plus Topics in Chapter 1 "Introduction to SAP"

Including

- SAP Introduction
- GTS
- GRC
- EHP
- Fiori
- Screen Personas
- Project Management
- System landscape
- Finance related Topics
- Hana

30 Plus Topics in Chapter 10 "Advance Tips and Tricks"

Including

- Variant Configuration
- 16 determinations shortcut
- SQVI (Table Join and reports)
- Debugging
- Pricing
- Table Edit
- LSMW
- Short Cuts (Parameters)
- EDI
- BAPI

Introduction to the Book

SAP Sales and Distribution Quick Configuration Guide focuses on very simple, easy to understand approach. The first chapter has simple and easy definitions so the reader can easily learn. Throughout the book, the reader will find very informative technological related definitions along with configuration step-by-step screenshots. Book was written to make reader grasp a better understand on configuration and some tricks.

I would encourage any feedback or comments on SAP Sales and Distribution Quick Configuration Guide by emailing rrizvir@gmail.com

Why This Book?

SAP Sales and Distribution Quick Configuration Guide is written with simplified definitions and in easy to follow steps with the latest related configuration of SAP Sales and Distribution.

Learning with Mind Maps:

Mind Map simplifies subjects to make the learning process easier. SAP Sales and Distribution Quick Configuration Guide uses mind map to introduce to introduce configuration.

Who can benefit from this Book?

- Consultants
- Business Analysts
- Managers
- Beginners

SAP Sales and Distribution Quick Configuration Guide is primarily written for anyone who is new to SAP Sales and Distribution configuration and wants to learn the basics. This book has basics in the first chapter that can help beginners and also refresh for experienced consultant.

This book is primarily written to learn SAP Sales and Distribution configuration with basics. This book can also benefit skilled consultant to utilize from configuration to subject understanding.

For feedback and comments rizvir at gmail and http://phtime.com/

CONTENTS

INTRODUCTION TO SAP   18

ENTERPRISE STRUCTURE   67

MASTER DATA   90

ORDER MANGMENT & CONTRACTS   125

DELIVERY & ROUTES   168

PRICING   184

BILLING & CREDIT MANAGEMENT   205

AVAILABLE TO PROMISE   228

LISTING / EXCLUSION & OUTPUT DETERMINATION   246

ADVANCED SAP TIPS & TRICKS WITH VC   260

CONTENTS

INTRODUCTION TO SAP **18**

Chapter One Topics 19

Introduction to SAP: 20

SAP Modules: 24

SAP Finance FICO: 25

MM Material Management / WM Warehouse Management 25

GTS and GTM 28

SAP GRC: 29

SAP Configuration: 29

OSS Notes: 29

EHP: 30

SAP Fiori: 30

SAP Personas: 30

Project: 30

Project Methodology: 31

Project Phases 31

Project Issue / Opportunity Management: 32

Issue Log: 33

Project Risk Management: 33

PMO: 33

Project complete life cycle: 34

SOW: 34

Basic Terms and Definitions: 36

SOA: 36

IT Infrastructure: 37

Rationale Document: 37

ERP: 37

Enterprise: 39

ECC: 39

Service Pack: 39

System Landscape: 39

ALV: 42

BAPI: 42

Field: 45

Data in SAP: 48

Node: 48

EDI: 48

IDOC: 48

SQL: 49

ANSI: 49

BASIS: 49

Instance: 49

Server: 49

IP address: 49

Object: 50

Synchronous: 50

Asynchronous: 50

AR (Account Receivable) and AP (Account Payment): 50

Accrual and cash Basis Accounting: 50

Profit Center: 50

Business process: 50

Cost Center: 51

Process Flow Diagram: 51

Workflow: 52

Use case: 52

General Ledger Accounting: 53

T-Account: 53

WBS: 54

Journal entry: 54

Credit 54

Debit 54

Debit and Credit: 55

T-code: 55

SAP Consultant: 56

OCM: 56

Stake Holder: 56

Big Data 57

Hana 57

SAP Easy Access Menu: 57

ASAP Implementation Methodology: 60

Project Preparation: 60

Objective: 61

Blueprinting: 61

Blueprint Documents: 62

Realization: 63

Go-live Preparation and Go-live 63

Best Practices: 64

"Z" and "Y" customization: 64

Summary Chapter 1 65

ENTERPRISE STRUCTURE **67**

Enterprise structure...69

Implementation Guide Customization:..71

Client:...72

Company:..72

Company Code:..73

Credit Control Area:...73

Sales Organization:..75

Distribution Channel:...76

Division:...77

Sales Area:...78

Sales Office:...79

Sales Group:...79

Plant:...80

Shipping Point:...81

Business Area:..82

Business Area determination:..83

Business Area Determine Plant and Item Division:...83

Business Area Determine by Sales Area:..84

Validation Of enterprise Structure:...85

Chapter 2 Summary...86

Exercise on Enterprise structure:..87

MASTER DATA
MASTER DATA **90**

Topics of Master Data Chapter:...91

Master Data:..92

Transactional Data:..92

Customer Master Data:..92

Contact Person partner function:..101

Customer Master Customization:..101

Account Group Customization:..101

Customer Partner Function Determination:...105

Common Distribution Channel:..108

Common Division:..109

Vendor Master SAP MM:...109

Material Master:..110

Material Type:..113

Customer Material Info Records..114

Payment Terms:...115

Payment Plan of Payment Term:...116

SAP SD Material Determination:..117

Maintain Table for Material Substitution:...118

Maintain Access Sequence:...118

Condition Type:...119

Material determination Procedure: 119

Material Deamination Condition Record: 122

Chapter 3 Summary: 123

ORDER MANGMENT & CONTRACTS 125

Chapter 4: Topics 126

Contract 127

Quantity Contract: 127

Value Contract: 127

Service Contract: 128

Master Contract: 128

Scheduling Agreement: 128

Rebate Agreement: 129

Sales Order Configuration 130

Sales Document Block: 132

Indicator: 132

Number Range: 133

General Control: 133

Scheduling Agreement: 136

Shipping: 137

Billing: 138

Sales Order Screenshots: 142

Item Category Customization: 145

Item Type: 148

Completion Rule: 148

Item Category Group: 149

Item category Determination: 149

Schedule Line: 151

Schedule Line Determination: 153

SAP Return Process RMA 154

Consignment Process: 155

The Consignment Issue 156

Plant Determination in Sales Order 157

Dynamic Item Proposal: 160

Customer Item Proposal Procedure: 160

Customer Product Proposal procedure Assignment: 161

Document Item Proposal Procedure: 161

Assignment of Document Procedure of Sales Document Type 161

Maintain Table of Origin for Product Proposal: 162

Define Product Proposal Procedure: 163

Procedure Determination for Background Processing: 164

Procedure Determination for Online Processing: 164

Item Proposal 165

Item proposal Customization: 166

Chapter 4 summary 167

DELIVERY & ROUTES 168

Delivery Customization 169

Delivery Type 170

Route Determination 171

Mode of Transport: 171

Define Shipment Type: 171

Define Transportation Connection Point: 172

Define Routes and stages: 172

Define Stages For All Routes: 174

Route Determination 174

Define Transportation Zone 175

Define Transportation Zone for shipping point & Country. 176

SAP SD Sales order Requirement Monitoring 177

Delivery and Reports on Delivery 177

Shipping Point Determination: 179

Chapter 5 summary 182

PRICING 184

Chapter 6 overview 185

SAP SD Pricing Fundamentals: 186

Condition Technique 186

Condition Technique: 186

Pricing Customization 187

Pricing Table: 187

Access Sequence: 188

Condition Type: 189

Additional Pricing Controls with Limits: 193

Pricing Procedure: 194

Pricing Procedure Determination: 197

Pricing with System Performance consideration: 199

Condition Record: 199

Field Catalog 201

SAP Pricing Routines: 201

Pricing in Order to cash: 202

Summary for Chapter 6 203

BILLING & CREDIT MANAGEMENT 205

Chapter 7 Topics 206

Introduction to Billing: 207

General Controls 208

Controls for Cancelation of billing document: 210

Controls for Account Assignment / Pricing 210

Output / Partner and Texts Controls: 210

Invoice List 211

Copy Control for Billing Document: 211

Billing Plans 213

Milestone Billing: 213

Periodic Billing: 214

Credit Management: 215

Credit reports and functionalities 217

Revenue Account Determination: 218

Accrued Revenue: 218

Deferred revenue: 218

Revenue Recognition Configuration: 219

Account Determination Configuration: 220

Master Data Account Group: 220

Decadency for account Determination: 221

Define Access Sequence and Account Determinations Type: 221

Define and assign account determination procedure: 222

Define and Assign Account Keys 223

Assign G/L Accounts: 223

Posting Period: 225

Chapter 7 Summary 226

AVAILABLE TO PROMISE **228**

Chapter summary 229

SAP SD Production Order MRP and ATP 230

Available to Promise and Availability Check: 231

How do master data affect MRP? 232

What is Requirement Type? 232

Transfer of requirement 232

Availability check: 232

ATP: 232

Allocation: 233

AC based on Planning: 233

Chapter 8 Summary 244

LISTING / EXCLUSION & OUTPUT DETERMINATION **246**

Output Determination: 247

Output Configuration: 248

Output Type Table: 248

Output Type Access Sequence:...249

Output Condition Type:..249

Output type Partner Function Assignment:...250

Output Determination Procedure:..251

Output Determination Procedure Assignment:..251

Text Determination...252

Define Text Type:..252

Define Access Sequence..254

Define Text Determine Procedure..254

Listing / Exclusion...255

Listing and Exclusion Customization:...255

Listing and Exclusion Access Sequence:..256

Listing and Exclusion Condition Type:..256

Listing and Exclusion Procedure:..256

Listing and Exclusion Activate sales document Type:..257

Chapter 9 Summary...258

ADVANCED SAP TIPS & TRICKS WITH VC...260

SAP Sales and Distribution Determinations:...261

SAP EDI..262

User Exit:...264

BADI:...265

How to Get BADI?...266

SAP SD Rebate Process and configuration..269

LSMW:...271

Master and Transactional Data Migration to SAP (add in data migration) 272

Cross matching for Duplicates..272

Looking Up T-codes...274

Mass Update:..276

Maintaining Pricing:..277

BAPI:..279

Condition Technique used at following configuration:...280

Third party drop ship...280

Variant:..281

SQVI:..282

Edit Table Entry:..283

Debugging ABAP program:..284

Variant Configuration:..285

Variant Configuration Sales and Distribution:...285

Material Master:..287

Class:...290

Characteristic..291

Pricing Characteristic..292

Variant Configuration, Pricing:..294

Following steps:..295

Configuration Profile:...295

Dependency:...295

Variant Configuration Trick:...297

Configuration related Icons..299

Parameters and less clicks:..299

Startup Transaction:...301

SAP ICONS:..302

Reports:...304

Table View:...305

Table View Old (SE16)..305

New Table View (SE16N):..306

Interface:..307

Chapter 10 Summary 308

Disclaimer:

This publication contains references to the products of SAP AG.

SAP, R/3, SAP NetWeaver, Duet, PartnerEdge, ByDesign, SAP BusinessObjects Explorer, StreamWork, and other SAP products and services mentioned herein as well as their respective logos are trademarks or registered trademarks of SAP AG in Germany and other countries. Business Objects and the Business Objects logo, Business Objects, Crystal Reports, Crystal Decisions, Web Intelligence, Xcelsius, and other BusinessObjects products and services mentioned herein as well as their respective logos are trademarks or registered trademarks of Business Objects Software Ltd. Business Objects is an SAP company. Sybase and Adaptive Server, iAnywhere, Sybase 365, SQL Anywhere, and other Sybase products and services mentioned herein as well as their respective logos are trademarks or registered trademarks of Sybase, Inc. Sybase is an SAP company. SAP AG is neither the author nor the publisher of this publication and is not responsible for its content. SAP Group shall not be liable for errors or omissions with respect to the materials. The only warranties for SAP Group products and services are those that are set forth in the express warranty statements accompanying such products and services, if any. Nothing herein should be construed as constituting an additional warranty.

This book is written by Syed Rizvi with his own personal views and understanding; it is not representing any company, products, and registered trademarks. The author does not assume any responsibility, error, and omissions and the book is based on "AS-IS". All the screenshots are copyright by SAP AG. This publication expresses no warranty, damages, guaranty, and liability whatsoever professional or any kind, direct or indirect. This book does not express warranty or guaranty, articulated or indirect to the accurateness or comprehensiveness of any information published herein of any kind.

Notes

CHAPTER 1

INTRODUCTION TO SAP

Chapter 1: Introduction to SAP ERP

Chapter One Topics :

- Introduction to SAP
- SAP Modules Introduction
- Project Methodology
- Basic term and Definitions
- Project Methodology
- Project Phases
- Project Issues Management
- Risk Management
- Project Manager
- Project complete life cycle
- Statement of work

First chapter has brief overview of SAP ERP and SAP Sales and Distribution related topics.

Introduction to SAP:

SAP AG is a name a of German software company. SAP stands for **S**ystem **A**pplication **P**roduct in data processing. It is enterprise software that is used by most of the fortune 500 companies. SAP ERP has a module for each department of the business. The modules are distinct, independent sections of business department representation of functions. SAP Modules are integrated so the data is more consistent and centralized in organization. SAP ERP system is divided into integrated modules for separate departmental for segregation of functions. The modules are integrated with each other so business departments can use a single record of the system centrally. SAP ERP is a suite of integrated modules together to accommodate business process. The modules are designed specifically for the industry with best practices and "industry standard". Aberration is used specifically to the special version of ERP system called "IS", like "IS-Retail" is designed out of SAP specify for retail industry. SAP provides special industry specific solutions. The following are examples of the IS solutions:

IS-Retail
IS-Oil and Gas
IS-Auto

The industry-centric solution provides in-depth features and functions that can benefit the system readiness with less enhancements. IS-Auto industry has solutions in parts suppression, VIN tracking the whole life cycle of VIN management and much more. SAP Out of the box requires customization according to the company's needs and also it has all the industry best practice integrated into it. SAP has suites of software products available other than SAP ERP. SAP ERP's latest version is called "**SAP ECC ERP**" and it stands for ERP **Central Component**. SAP ERP is a three-tier based system with each tier representing each section of the software application.

- **Application (Application Server)**
- **Presentation (Computer, mobile, web, etc.)**
- **Database (Database server)**

Subsequent Figure Present the three tier system.

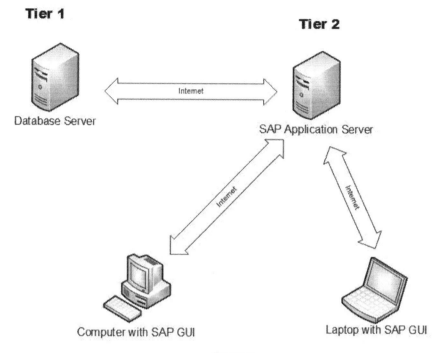

Figure 1

- **Application Server**
- **Database Server**
- **GUI** (Graphical User Interface)

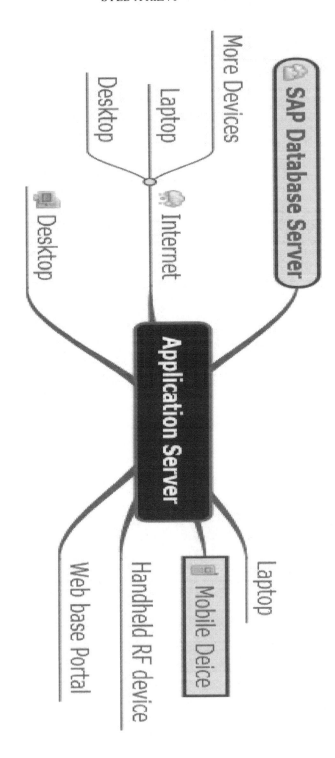

Figure 2

Application:

Very Important

The SAP Application server is part of the R/3 architecture. A server is a physical machine which has multiple processors to handle multiple programs at a time or it could be a virtual server. A SAP Application server is accessed via the GUI. The server can connect with many devices to the presentation tier and it is also connected with SAP database server, completing the three tier systems of SAP ERP R/3.

Presentation:

Presentation usually is the SAP GUI software to install on computer or laptop. GUI stands for graphical user interface. Presentation tier can be used via mobile or web browser. The device that is connected to the application server via GUI or web or mobile device is called presentation.

Database:

The database is a collection of tables. When we collect many tables together on same sever its called database. The collection of tales are saved in the database server. The database server could be one server or could be a group of servers that represent the database. The SAP ERP database server typically has a separate server.

SAP Modules:

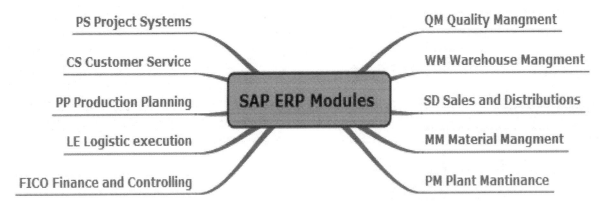

Figure 3

SAP application is a solution for enterprise. That being said, enterprise consists of many departments. Any business could be divided into three main units:

- Accounting
- Logistics
- Human resource

These departments also can be divided into many more sub divisions. The sub division of these main unite of business is represented as modules in SAP. Each module could be standalone implemented by the business and it requires integration with their existing system and other departmental systems. One of reasons SAP ERP leader in market is that all of SAP modules are integrated and communicates to each other seamlessly, some example of the SAP module are followed:

- FI Finance
- CO Controlling
- SD Sales and Distribution
- MM Material Management
- LE Logistic execution
- PP Production Planning

SAP Finance FICO:

FICO stands for finance and controlling (modules). SAP and FICO are two different modules, but are integrated with each other. Each business entity requires accounting setup for the legal and internal process: The functions are general ledger reporting, tax, account receivable, account payable, and so on. The FI module has a factory calendar, GL General Leger account, chart of account, company code (separate entity), reconciliation account, account payable, account, and receivable account groups among more functions. Integration point of SAP SD and SAP FI are at the sales order level at sales, customer master payment method and, payment term; it also integrates at for credit management for customer credit master. SAP FICO Finance integrates at account determinations, revenue determination, cost center, and costing.

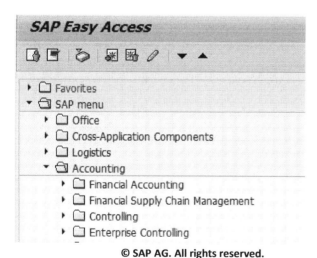

Figure 4

MM Material Management / WM Warehouse Management

Material management is part of logistics. It involves inventory and purchasing process, subcontracting, procurement, etc.

The warehouse management module comes under the material management module. It is a sub-part of the Material Management module. In WM module it has major activities involved in Plant and warehouse related transactions. The processes under WM are, cycle counting, Inventory Management, Transfer Order, Picking Order, Picking, Packing, Handling unit, etc.

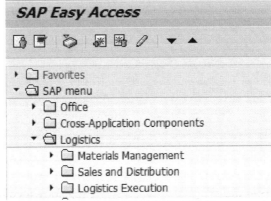

Logistic Execution:

The SAP Logistic Execution module integrates with sales and distribution along with the material management module. The distribution channel is one of the integration points between SAP SD and logistic execution the enterprise structure configuration is in the logistic execution area. The in order to cash cycle delivery document is another point of integration with Logistic execution. Delivery inbound and outbound process come under logistic execution. The following are a few of logistic execution related functionalities:

- Inbound Delivery
- Outbound Delivery
- Warehouse Management
- Shipping
- Yard Management

SAP Sales and Distribution:

Very Important

SAP Sales and distribution module have functionalities which it consists of sales related activities. In sales, functionalities include Inquiry, Quotation, Contracts, Pricing, Sales Orders, Billing, Rebate, and many more.

Pricing is one of the complex functions of sales and distribution module, supporting many scenarios to be handled. Pricing is also used in the material management module with the same basic principle.

Sales order management and configuration controls, Inquiry, quotation, order on key areas of Sales and Distribution module.

Delivery is in the integrated areas of the logistic execution module including the sales and distribution stand point customization of outbound delivery.

Billing is integrated with finance and part of SAP SD invoice areas. Billing account determination and bling plans are customized.

Credit Management relates to the customer master data setup and also finance integrated area to setup credit master.

To view sales and distribution related T-codes:

VA00 will bring only sales related menu from an easy access menu
VF00 will display all billing related t-codes

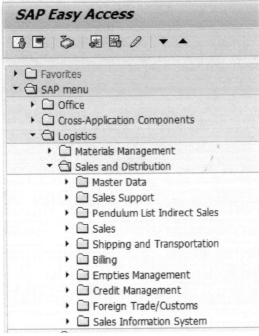

PP Production Planning:

The PP module provides product production planning, controlling, and scheduling. It involves, bill of material, long term planning, demand management, material requirement planning, capacity planning, production orders, and KANBAN process.

GTS and GTM

SAP Sales and Distribution have standard trade compliance functionality, which is outdated and limited. SAP GTS and GTM modules have full range of functionality with industry standards best practices. SAP GTS stands for Global Trade Compliance. SAP GTM stands for Global Trade Management. SAP GTM manages compliance from the standpoint of globally. SAP GTS integrates for logistics and financial area to custom compliances. SAP GTS provides functions including the following:

- Denied Party screening (Customer Master)
- Sanction Country Screening (in transactions, order, delivery, invoice)
- Screening on Products License (Material Master)
- Denied Freight forwarder screening (Vendor Master)
- Dangerous goods

- Harmonized tariff code management
- Drawback functionality

SAP GTS provides for custom related government compliance controls, so corporations stay up to date with regulations and avoid fines and penalties. SAP GTM part of ERP and SAP GTS is part of GRC.

SAP GRC:

SAP GRC stands for Global Risk and Compliance. SAP GRC software is SAP product which is used for the following areas:

- Financial Compliance
- Trade Management
- Environmental Regulations
- User provisioning, roles and authorization

Financial Compliance includes SOX, Roles, fraud, and risk related processes. Trade management includes ITAR and EAR compliance.

SAP Configuration:

SAP out of the box requires setup called building blocks also as per business senior and function activations. Building blocks are used to setup which is essential to have baseline the system. SAP provides OSS notes and documentation for the OSS notes and building block. Configuration for the transactions setup which also come under the term of configuration. System is configured as per business process requirements. Based on the configuration functions of the transactions get impacted and get manipulated. Configuration is done by experienced consultants. If the configuration is not done with SAP recommendations and intelligent design, it can affect performance, complexity, and difficulty for the end user transaction. To configure system, the T-code is: SPRO which is also called IMG. IMG stands for Implementation Guide. Configuration is also called customization.

OSS Notes:

OSS note stands for **O**nline **S**ervice **S**ystem. It is the SAP support system. If SAP version has SAP support valid, then SAP will provide support for bugs or issues through OSS. One can look at existing OSS notes and apply the solution accordingly. SAP OSS notes can be downloaded and applied via T-code SNOTE. SAP OSS notes available on sap support website. Also, OSS notes available for known issues and their solutions so those not also help before we can open a ticket with SAP. To view OSS, note user need S-ID which is SAP issued id related to the system.

EHP:

EHP stands for Enhancement Pack. Each version of SAP comes with many enhancement packs. Enhancement pack provides new features and upgrades to the latest version of SAP ERP ECC.

The latest version of SAP ERP ECC 6.0 enhancement pack "SAP ECC 6.0 **EHP 7.0**"

SAP Fiori:

SAP Fiori UX is a sap revived application which gears toward new user experience. It provides a mobile web base use of ERP functions. SAP Fiori is a bundle of applications for the enterprise with User interface and customize functions for user specific needs. It is compatible with mobile devices and is easy to customize. SAP Fiori web base application allows access for mobile device and tablets. SAP Fiori has released set of application based on ERP module's functionality.

For more information http://help.sap.com/fiori_products#section1

SAP Personas:

SAP Personas is screen customization application. It is built for ERP GUI customization. With customization transactions can be customized, scripts can be incorporated into buttons and shortcuts. The background, buttons, themes, and colors can be totally customized as easy as drag and drop. It introduced by SAP and will affect all the SAP products for a design change.

Project:

Important

Any strategy or planning that has start and end date can be categorized as a project. Project has project plan, project scope, and resources. Project is executed with interrelated activities with Project implementation methodology. The Project Methodology examples are ASAP and Agile.

Project Methodology:

Important ▪▪▪▪

What is Methodology? Methodology is systematic, organized proven model, method, or implementing objectives. Methodology is model of work which has been tested and performed many times for expected results. Methodology is being used in many fields for expected result in a controlled manner. Use of methodology ensures the expected result from desire projects. Use of methodology is proven in many areas to achieve success in calculating manner.

By using Methodology one can be expect a predictable result. Methodology can be effective if followed completely, otherwise it becomes harmful because a new way of implementation is different. Methodology has set of rules and parameters with the phase-wise approach. Based on industry best practices, one methodology can be more effective as compared to another methodology.

Example of methodologies:

- Implementation methodology
- Business modeling methodology
- Research Methodology

Due to validation by industry, methodology use will be one of the deciding factors for controlling the outcome. If we do not follow the methodology, then trial and error are unpredictable and can be uncontrolled in nature. When individuals or organization deviates from methodology, then that will put risk in a project, and often time it is human error.

Project Phases

Very Important ▪▪▪▪

3. Realization Phase

1. Project Prepration

4. Go live preparation Phase

ASAP Project Methodology

2. Blue printing

Support

5. Go Live Phase

What is Project phase? Project Phase means limited or defined period of time. The project is divided into phases. In project phases, particular activities are defined for the each phase. The activities and targets need to be achieved before the next phase.

SAP ASAP Methodology

1. **Project preparation Phase**
2. **Blueprint phase**
3. **Realization Phase**
4. **Go live preparation Phase**
5. **Go Live Phase**

Each phase has deliverable and set of activities to consider and complete each phase. Certain methodologies use more phases and small, iterative cycles to achieve goals. For example "Agile" mythology has small iterative cycles. What is a project cycle? Project cycle means beginning to end of projects from the first phase to the last phase of the project. Each phase of the project requires complete team work with interrelated activities.

Project Issue / Opportunity Management:

Very Important ▪▪▪▪▪

What is the issue and what is the risk? The issue is already happening. Risk is future state that is going to happen; it might create a problem later point of time. Every issue is an opportunity for correction. The risk and issue logs should be available to project team and business team to update. If these logs are not available to the project team to update, then that can become a more problematic. If issue and risk from the team are not logged, then the assumption and ignorance of this issue will affect later point of time in the project.

Issue Log:

Very Important

Issue means it is currently on hand. Project issue log should be followed by a project managed to solve the team's issue. In my opinion, anyone should be able to create an issue log and update the issue log. All issues should be followed properly and address properly. Many tools can be used to manage issue log, including software's and tracking sheets.

Project Risk Management:

Very Important

Risks are predictions of coming issues. The Risk could be identified in any phase of the project. It is better to close the risk. The biggest risk is that when project managers, stakeholders, and team members ignore risks.

PMO:

PMO stands for Project Management Office or officer. Each project has PMO. In general there is one Project manager from customer side and one project manager from the vendor side. There could be multiple Project managers on both sides to accommodate the project. Project manager's responsibility is to manage resources, scope and delivery.

Project complete life cycle:

Moderately Important ▬◼◼◼

What is a project? The project has started and end dates. Based on the project timelines, it has particular goals and objects which need to be achieved. The best way to achieve these targets is to use methodology. After successfully completing all of the required activities from all of the phase's project ends and that completes the life cycle of the project.

SOW:

Important topic ▬◼◼◼

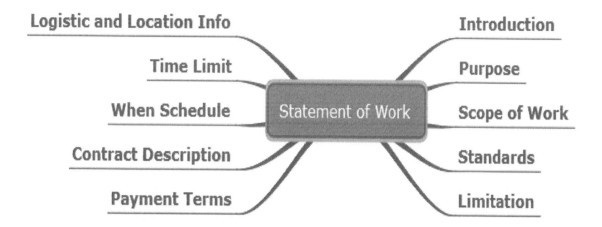

Logistic and Location Info — Introduction
Time Limit — Purpose
When Schedule — **Statement of Work** — Scope of Work
Contract Description — Standards
Payment Terms — Limitation

Introduction:

SOW stands for a statement of work. It is a legally binding document / engagement / service contract, etc. SOW is the short form of Statement of work. SOW is result of a bidding process from request for quotation and request for personal process in between companies to singe a contract. SOW contains details of project durables score, start and end date, contract type, pricing, compliance, and detail terms and conditions.

Description:

Statement of work is the contrast between software services providing company. It contains project deliverable. SOW provides a project team basis to work on, and then that durables will reflect on the project plan. SOW has high levels of information regarding project durables. It requires project manager and team members to consider according to SOW and project plan. During the project if new requirement is introduced by business, then SOW will require a change request. With a change request SOW requires version management and its effects on project plan and subsequently resources and scope.

Lesson learned Project Experience:

Lesson learned from previous project what mistakes has been done and what we learned from it.

Important

Any projected objective that is managed under boundaries of time, resource, and scope can be considered a project. Many methodologies are used as per recommendation of system integrators and experts. System Integrator is a reference to the contracting company who come as contractors to implement, upgrade, or rollout project. There could be one or multiple system integrators in the project.

Origin of Project:
Where do project starts from? The need for the improvement, innovation, dealing with existing issues, system limitation, and compliance can be one of the reasons for the project. The original need is presented to the stakeholder and higher management for the approval and project scope is born out of the approval.

Business Project Task:
The project statement should be documented in detail so the project original statement should not be confused later on or get off track. In often much time the original goal of the project is not planned as it should be cast off.

Reason of the Scope Issue:
When the scope is left to the whole team and system Integrator is decide then it can get out of control when it is not funneling down to one person. The most important fact is that, what is project statement, why project was started for? Scope should carefully decide for the project and should be echoed in every project document. The big companies like Google and Facebook could be great examples. They have an open door policy for ideas and issues so the new ideas will be challenged so it can be tested in production.

Important

Basic Terms and Definitions:

The term and definitions are essential to learn prior to learn SAP Sales and Distribution or SAP in general. It is important to understand the terms.

SOA:

SOA stands for Service Orientated architecture. It is software architecture, complete designer element or representing solution for large process into the software development process.

IT Infrastructure:

This is referred to a physical server and network setup of the organization. It contains server software, data centers, network, etc. IT infrastructure also refers to hardware or software infrastructure.

Rationale Document:

A document that contains pictorial a representation with step-by-step instructions is called a rational document. Rationale document could have few or all of these elements: Definitions, instructions, screenshots, procedures, different organization, and customization and design documents with their requirements. This document also can be used for a training document. Depending on the organization they call the document different names.

ERP:

Representation of ERP in mind map.

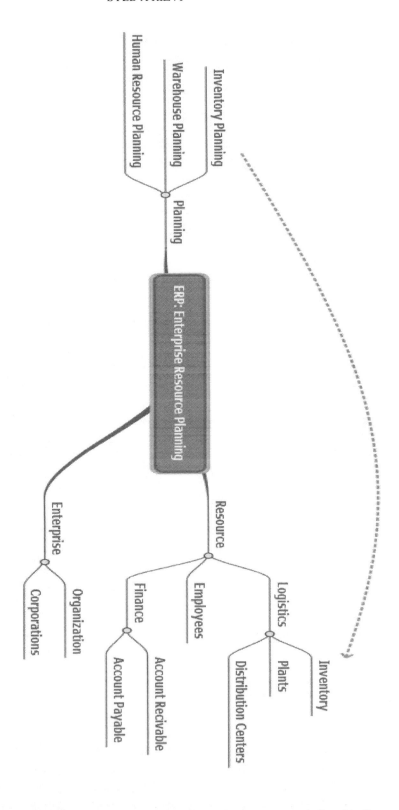

ERP Stands for Enterprise Resource Planning. Few of ERP functions are defined in figure, how enterprise resource planning works. Many business departments are managed by the organization, so ERP software become a necessity that can handle multiple departments and resources centrally.

Enterprise:

Enterprise represents a business or organization. Any big organization with big departments or many departments can be called enterprise.

ECC:

ECC stands for ERP central Component. ECC abbreviation is used by SAP to identify its new release of SAP. Usually ECC is used for version SAP ERP 5.0 ECC OR SAPERP 6.0.

Service Pack:

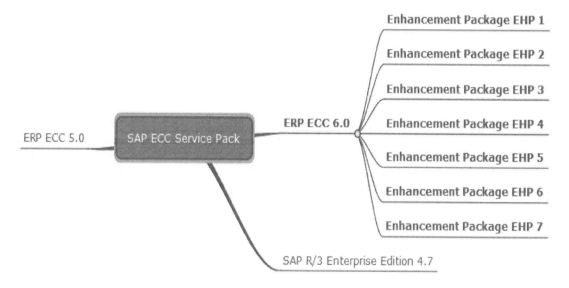

Service pack refers to upgrades to specific version of SAP. The reason for service pack could be based on bug fix and additional features.

System Landscape:

In general, system landscapes have three identical environments. In project, we develop functions in "development system" and then it is transported to the "quality server" for testing. After testing is done, it will be transported to "production system". The sandbox also can be "development system" or separate system. It depends on company to company how they want to set system landscape and maintain how many environments.

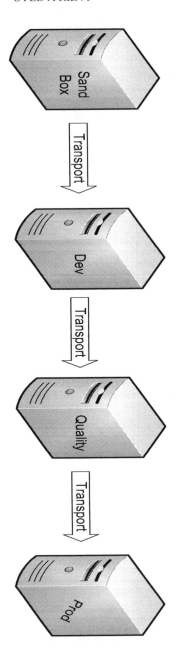

System Landscape

The system landscape consists of separate SAP server instances identical and has connectivity for transport requests in between them. In general, system landscapes consist of three system environments:

1. Development
2. Quality
3. Production

Development System:

The development system is used for system configuration and custom development. There can be a multiple development systems ranging from different clients. Particular users have selected roles and access to the system. The customization change assigned to transportation request and these customized objects are transported via transport to quality for further testing.

Quality System:

In Quality environment efforts are spent on testing. In quality system users run test scripts. The quality system is utilized for "user acceptance testing" and "regression testing". Quality environment is there to check the quality of configuration and custom development testing.

Production System:

Live systems used by business for transections are called production system. Changes to the production system are very limited. For new functions, developments are only allowed in sandbox. The quality system transport is for any object after the process of approval and successful test cycle. Production system require data migration data before go-live. The production system is used by end users after go-live.

Process:

Process is an activity which takes inputs, adds value to it, or changes it and produce outputs from it.

ABAP:

ABAP stands for Advance Business Application Programing. ABAP is used in SAP to change or enhance the SAP standard. ABAP programming language is the basis of SAP programs. To understand ABAP programing, use the following t-codes. These t-codes also provide examples how to use the syntax in programing.

T-code: ABAPHELP
T-code: ABAPDOCU

ALV:

ALV stands for ABAP list viewer. Most of SAP reports have an ALV option to select different variations and selection options for the data to display. With this, users can hide, display, or suppress fields or header and item level information into report. It is very flexible tool for the reports.

BAPI:

BAPI stands for Business Application Programing Interface. BAPI also called the functional module. BAPI is the programming which enables transaction or master data relevant functionality for interface users.

Document:

In past and still in present, Paper documents are used for record keeping. Today records are saved in a computer files called an electronic document. In computers and servers all electronic files are saved in database as electronic documents. The electronic document is divided into three sections.

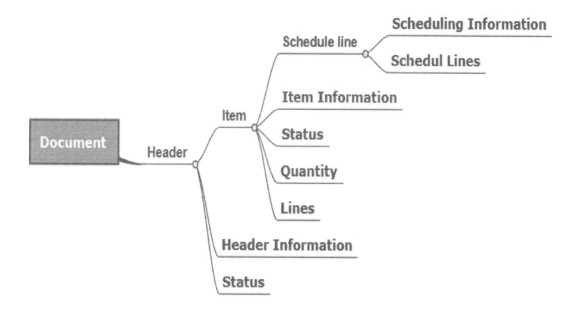

The document represents information or proof record or record.
In SAP document have three parts

1. **Header**
2. **Item**
3. **Schedule Line**

The header represents a controlling point of the document, item represents the content of document, and schedule line is indicating it has a particular action at the end of a document.

In SAP SD, each document could have two to three sections like billing document, only having a header and item data information in it.

SAP SD document types:

1. **Sales Document**

   Header Data
   Item Data
   Schedule Line Data

2. **Billing Document**

   Header Data
   Item Data

Header Data:

Header data defines the type of the document. It controls the behavior of the document.

Item Data:

Item data contains header data and it contains Item data. Each line data has the same header.

Schedule Line Data:

Schedule Line Data contains scheduling information of a document.

Database:

Very Important

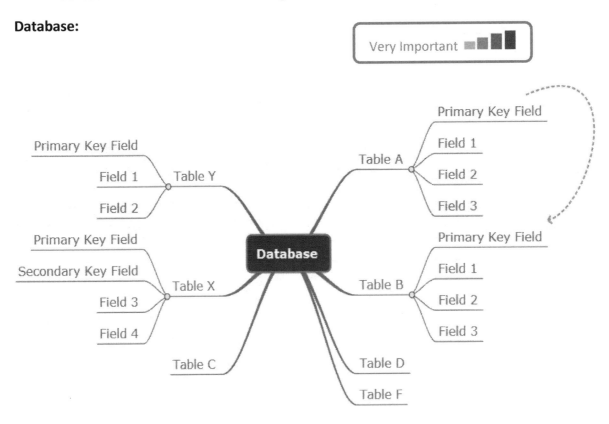

The database is a repository or collection of tables. The table is consisting of rows and columns. Database is managed in database servers.

Number Range:

Number range controls the number of master or transactional data. Number range is a SAP configuration for transactional or master data. Number range is used in different transactions, but mainly two types of number ranges exist:

1. **internal number range**
2. **External Number Range**

Internal number range can be used for sales orders numbers, customer master, master data objects, or other transactions. It can be auto generated by the system. The internal number range configured as per customizing object. The external number range means that user can use own number in the transaction.

Table:

Very Important

Table represents data in in structural way. Tables contain information in rows and columns. Data is used for programs and software. Where row and column intersect it called a field. In SAP, data is used for master data to transactional data. It is very important to understand. SAP has very large numbers of tables. Each field has its characteristics, for example character types (Numbers or Alphabets) are allowed for what is the length is allowed in the field. These are all information and settings of a table are stored in "Data type". Every table has header data to distinguish this table from other tables and program use.

Every table has one or more key fields. The key field in the table is used to make a connection in data table to data table or make sure unique row of data. The purpose of key field to identify same key filed to lookup data in other tables for relevant information and able to bread big data to able to use with less complex and big data into pieces. In SAP tables are system defined tables and SAP allow user to create customer tables. Tables can be created with T-code SE11.

Key Field ID#	First Name	Last Name	DOB
78692110	Ali	Zer	01/01/82
78692111	Sibtay	Jaffer	02/02/65

SAP has header and item tables for different transection and master data.

Header table and item table connect with each other with key field.

Field:

A field is located at rows and Colum intersection. Each field has properties for a header field. In other words, if a header field is date then for each record following this field will be dated so data will stay consistent. So each field has many controls behind it. Field characteristic defines at header level. The following are several values of the field.

- Field Name
- Technical Name
- Key Field
- Data Element
- Data Type
- Length
- Decimal Place
- Short Description

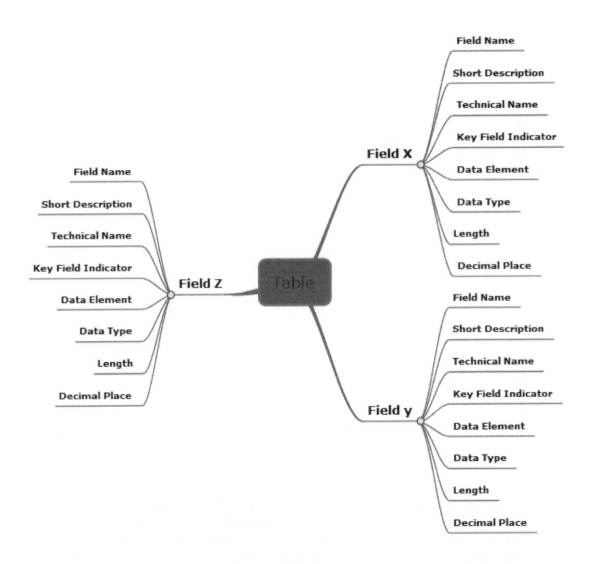

Field Status Group:

SAP has four field statuses and it called field status group:

1. Required
2. Suppressed
3. Optional
4. Display

With this control, if allowed, each field can be displayed, hidden, suppressed, or optional in master data or transactional data. The required field status is mandatory field. The suppressed field option is used to hide the field. The optional field property is used to keep field optional to use or leave it empty.

Display:
Display status of the field only displays the content, it cannot be changed. When field status is on display status it only displays the content of the field.

Suppress:
Suppress means hiding the field from the screen on the master data or transaction data processing.

Optional:
Optional field status is used to be available as an option. When field status is an optional, the user can fill the data or leave it empty in data processing.

Required:

Required field status is the status of the field to make it required in data processing. When filed is on required status, the transaction can be processed unless required entry is filled.

Data in SAP:

The system has two types of data.

1. **Master Data**
2. **Transactional data**

Master Data:

The data that hardly changes and used in transection as basis for the transactions.

Example and more information:

The name and address of a person can consider master data. The name of a person hardly changes. The address can be master data, and it changes rarely too. In SAP master data has many fields to represent it detail. Master data are based on the enterprise structure.

Transactional Date:

The data that changes often called transactional data. It is based on master data with variations with transactions. The sales document, delivery and billing document very good example of transactional data.

Node:

Node refers to computer, server, or group of servers. The node is used in networking terms to define the system.

EDI:

EDI stands for Electronic Data Interface. EDI is the way that data get flow between which is EDI capable to transmit and receive files between them. EDI is industry standard to send and receive EDI orders, invoices, delivery, and other transactions to do business.

IDOC:

IDOC stands for Intermediate Document. IDOC's made for EDI interface and interfaces. IDOCS can be viewed with t-code IDOC. IDOC also can be used for data migration too with LSMW.

SQL:

SQL stands for Structured Query Language, it is database related. SQL uses to call tables and data using SQL commands. It is based on ANSI.

ANSI:

ANSI stands for the American National Standards Institute. ANSI help in the development of standard for more information, please go to the link http://www.ansi.org.

BASIS:

Basis refers to the SAP system admin and security module. Basis Consultant install, upgrade, maintain, security, and administer the system. The basis consultant is not the ABAP programmer. The basis consultant involves in role and authorization setup related activities in project and in system support. It also upgrades system and enhancement pack.

Instance:

Just like a Node instance is referring to single computer, server, or group of server define at one Instance.

Server:

The server is a computer system that serves many computers, laptop, and mobile. The server software application has to serve single or group of systems. In general server has more processors, system memory, and network bandwidth to process.

IP address:

IP stands for Internet Protocol. An IP address is a unique address for each computer or network card. An IP address is issued against the unique Mac address on each network card.

Object:

Word object is also used as object oriented programming referring it to the single reusable piece of a program or library. The object is referring to section of complete set of program.

Synchronous:

Synchronous means real time data processing transaction. The good example of synchronous process is a phone call when data is synchronous between two or more phones. It is used in interface related document if the interface is synchronous.

Asynchronous:

Asynchronous is opposite of synchronous, it is not real time. For example, when the process involves periodic update then it considers asynchronous. It is used in interface related document if the interface is asynchronous. Good example is mail it take time to come.

AR (Account Receivable) and AP (Account Payment):

AR refers to accounts receivable, which is used in the revenue for the sales income. AP refers to accounts payable and is in the result of procurement when buy products or services and need to pay for them.

Accrual and cash Basis Accounting:

In accounting, revenue is calculated on the basis of either cash or Accrual. Accrual mean added up and keep track of it, on the accrual basis of accounting the amount is tracked and eventually it is posted for accounting purposes. Cash basis accounting it is posted as soon as the transaction is processed in the system or accounting.

Profit Center:

Profit center is related to accounting, it keeps track for profit and cost. Profit center is used in SAP finance and controlling module.

Business process:

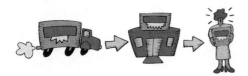

What is a business process? The Process has inputs and outputs with value added has to input. Any inputs are worked on and/or add value to it. From there it produces output that have added value to it or output is different from input, then it called process. Any process of business is called business process. For example, sales order creation is the business process.

Cost Center:

Cost center is an internal company account, which use for accounting purposes to add expense to it. Cost centers are used to put expense toward the account to track cost of departments. In general, cost centers are used for marketing, giveaway, research and development, and returns cost tracking.

Process Flow Diagram:

The pictorial representation of process is called "process flow diagram". Process box is, in rectangular shape, present one process and it has input and output. Each process has value added to call each box a process itself. The methodologies have many representation schema to represent process flow diagrams. The example of process flow diagram methodology is UML and BPMN. UML stands for Unified modeling language, and BPMN stands for Business Process Model Notation.

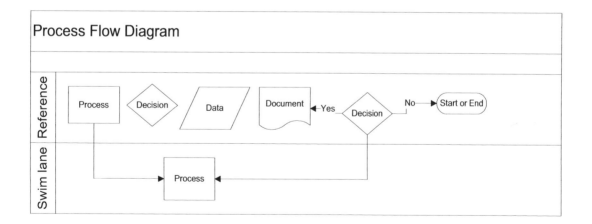

Business Process Methodology:

Business process methodology is the representation of business process, step by step with detailed information is captured on each process. The most common business process methodology is used are UML (Unified Modeling Language). Business Process methodology can be defined in different ways, but certain industry standards and methodologies are proven and become more effective. The two business notation methodologies are good example UML AND BPMN. UML stands for Unified modeling Language and BPMN stands for Business process Language.

Workflow:

The business process has a process of approvals for quality work and accountability. Workflow is a system of work that go through for business approvals and administration. Workflow is one of the key features available in SAP to check all available workflow documents to check status. Also in SAP, workflow is part of RECIFW that is counted toward system change other than the standard functionality of SAP ERP.

Use case:

Use case is a pictorial representation of process in framework of representation method. This will help for visual process flow to understand. The use case has Actors in stick figures interacting with system define in the middle. This is UML Methodology to represent use case. Use case is created as per requirement gathering and documentation for the project.

Use case diagram. It is simple diagram representing system and characters.

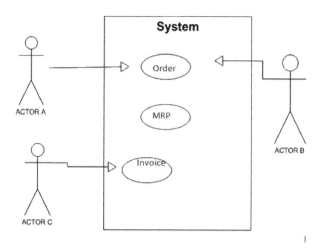

General Ledger Accounting:

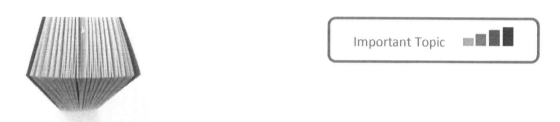

General ledger accounting is bookkeeping of business transactions for profit, loss report and all other financial purposes. It is very important for business to keep track of transaction for legal and accountability. The SAP has General ledger accounting integrated with all of the modules and it keeps track of all financial transactions.

T-Account:

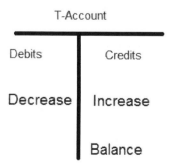

T-account used in accounting. It is used to define the account with

Journal entries. On left side of the T-account debit and right side credit. In the figure, we can see left side for debit and Right side is credited. At the end of T-account we can see balance from both sides of transactions and keep track of journal leader balance with sub T-accounts.

WBS:

WBS stands for Work Breakdown Structure. It is used in Projects to calculate work, time, and cost for the relating to the project. It is part of Module Project Systems (SAP PS) for internal order and project.

Journal entry:

In T-accounting each transaction is entered either on debit or credit called journal entry.

Credit

Very Important ▪▪▮▮

Credit means an increase in amount or gain. Credit refers to entry in accounting when balance increase. When we over pay our bill then we will receive credit balance transfer back.

Debit

Very Important ▪▪▮▮

In accounting, debit refers to decrease in account. For example, debit means to pay out something so it decreases amount transfer out of balance.

Debit and Credit:

Debit and credit means one party credit is an opposite party's debit. When we receive money it is credit and when we pay it is debited.

Credit and Debit memo

Credit and Debit memo is just a document that is refereeing the credit and debit in the document.

T-code:

T-code stands for transaction code. The easy access menu has transaction bar as we can see it in the screenshot. In this transection bar user enter T-code.

Tips to remember T-code:

Here are some tips to remember T-code alphabets.

Character	Description
N	Number
V	Sales
F	Billing
M	Material Master
01	Create
02	Changes
03	Display
05	Report

To get reports for any module from EASY Access Menu use T-code: **SAP1**
this will only show report from every module.

Sales related MENU use t-code: **VA00**

For Customization (Implementation Guide also abbreviated into IMG) T-code is: **SPRO**

/o	Open New Session
/n	To end the current transaction
/i	To delete the current session
/nend	To log off with saving
/nex	Exit without saving

SME:

SME stand for Subject Mater Expert. Subject matter expert is a title given to technology or business related knowledge.

SAP Consultant:

SAP Consultant is a title for the role in which his/her responsibilities fall into the project implementation or support role.

The responsibility of consulting differs based on organization, the role, and responsibility assigned to him/her, methodology, or organization structures of work.

OCM:

OCM stands for Organizational Change Management. Project implementation and business related tasks and process change OCM streams to help businesses be prepared for manageable transition into the new system. OCM teams work with management for organizational changes.

Stake Holder:

A stakeholder is an individual or group of individuals who are responsible for the project from the business side. The project manager reports to stake holders for project progress. Stakeholders can approve the additional scope of the project or remove it, based on project vision.

Big Data

Big data considered where an organization has huge data to be process and different tools are used for data warehousing and data processing. One of the big data product example is SAP BW or SAP HANA.

Hana

SAP HANA is SAP product for in memory data processing. SAP has developed product with HANA and service pack SAP ECC service pack EHP is HANA specific. Hana has much more faster data processing. SAP made their own database system where logic of data reading is different from traditional reading. It has better compatibility with web services and SAP Fiori.

SAP Easy Access Menu:

The SAP Easy Access Menu is the initial screen after logging into the SAP GUI. The Easy access menu can be customized with GUI options. In general SAP easy access menu can have six separate sessions running at the same time. The easy access menu has a transaction code bar for T-codes. The easy access menu can be customized and assigned to the user or group of users.

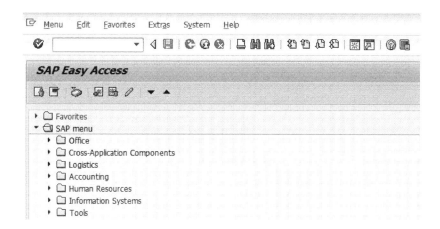

The easy access menu can be customized and assigned to the user or group of users.

Easy Access Menu buttons and shortcuts:

Button	Description	Shortcut
	Enter	
	Command Field for T-codes the triangle close the command field	
	Save	ctrl + S
	Back	F3
	Log Off (from current session)	Shift + F3
	Cancel	F12
	Print	Ctrl + P
	Find	Ctrl + F
	Find Next	Ctrl + G
	First Page	Ctrl + page up
	Page up	
	Page Down	
	Last Page	Ctrl + pg den
	New Session	

↗	Create shortcut	
?	Help	F1
	Customize Local Layout (change Color, themes, font size, etc.)	
	Add to Favorites	Ctrl + shift + F6
	Delete Favorite	Shift + F12
✎	Change Favorite	Ctrl + shift + F3

SAP Messages Types:

In SAP, error messages are defined in different categories. Some errors are not able to be passed and something have to be changed. If a warning that comes in red, it leans it is a hard error and cannot be ignored. Some errors are not hard errors, so they are called soft errors. The warning error is in yellow and it can be ignored, but the user sees warranting. In the event of the transaction system issues a message status of transection to user. In SAP, messages are defined in different categories with their following are the message types. Each process has a message type in SAP. It gives a status to the user for the success and failure:

1. Warring
2. Error
3. Exit
4. Success

Each process has a message type in SAP. It gives a status to the user for the success and failure.

Message Type	Screens hot	Description
Information		The message type is for information purpose, by clicking the icon it will open a new window with information.
Warning:		It has warned on next step it can be corrected before the warning is ignored. (The user can ignore it by pressing enter) The warning may appear more than once based on transactions. It appears on left bottom of the screen.
Hard Error		Message gives a hard stop. Unless the correction made, it will stay at error and will not process.
Exit		Message exits the trisections and gives a short dump, or stop the transaction.
Success		Success message with document number or if this transaction is successful this will appear. It appears on left bottom of the screen.

ASAP Implementation Methodology:

ASAP stands for Accelerated SAP. It is a project implementation methodology by SAP. It is cost effective, proven, and streamlined for SAP solution implementations if used as it is defined by SAP. It is also called SAP road-map implementation. The new version of ASAP is introduced by SAP, but the scope of this book to understand basics and brief introduction.

ASAP Methodology Roadmap divided into five major phases.

- **Project preparation**
- **Blueprinting**
- **Functional Developer or Realization**
- **Final Preparation or goes live preparation**
- **Go-live**
- **Support**

Project Preparation:

Very Important ▬▬■■

Project preparation involves getting ready for the project, commercial discussion, and finalization of SOW or updated.

Project Preparation involves:

- Team and stakeholder identification
- Role and responsibility assignment
- Team building activities
- Process of approval
- Scope and Objective

The scope of the project means what modules, functionalities, systems, and components for implementation. The scope should be very clear so everyone work on the same target. Team building activities are required in the discovery phase for team identifications.

Objective:

Based on the project preparation phase, the stakeholder requirement report is generated. This report is based on business scenarios and how the overall business is looking for their future state and innovations from the vision statement. The statement for starting the project should be the echo point for all other deliverables, so that the original project statement should not go off track.

Requirement Gathering involves capturing every point that a business requires and categorizing them according the type of the requirement. There are two parts of the requirement gathering. First is to write every single one of them and get validation on them. The second step is to match with system capability and evaluate if they are part of an existing system or not and what kind of enhancement it will be when further categorized. Then all of the requirements should be presented to the business with time estimates within the time limit.

The project scope is based on the project statement. Project statements derived from the business vision statement. It could be based on infrastructure or software-based requirement.

Blueprinting:

It starts from requirement gathering workshops. In workshops, business analyst, and consultant capture current processes. The captured business process needs to be analyzed for fit and gap analysis. The blueprint requirement gathering start from a standard SAP process and comparing AS-IS process to find fits and gaps and perform fit gap analysis. One of The outcome from blueprint is that blueprint document. Gap analysis is based on RICIFW: Reports, Interfaces, Conversions, Forms, Work flow. Few examples of deliverables from blue print phase are:

- Blueprint Documents
- Functional Specification Document

Blueprint Documents:

Many "headings" can be included in the blueprint document, but several useful topics that should be used are in template of the project documents. The following are some of the topics should be in a blueprint document. Every organization uses their own and use project standards. The following are some brief topics that should be in the blue print document. The functional specification document is also one of the deliverable of realization phase.

- AS-IS Business Process
- AS-IS process flow Diagram
- Pain points and requirements
- To-be process flow diagram
- To be process details
- Gap-analysis standard or GAP
- RECIF Process
- Business process owner and BA details
- Project name and doc version
- Status of the document with version history
- Roles and Security
- OCM Change Impact
- Feedback from Business

The blueprint should contain feedback from business and from project team members. The time and target date should be kept in the document so it would truly reflect the end date and completion date. The successful blueprint document should be easy to understand after all it will be read by business team not by the technical team.

Realization:

The major activities in realization phase are system configuration, testing, functional specification development, RECIF development, etc. Teams start from system configuration and enhancements. For testing, a test script is executed with test plans and scenarios. The deliverables for testing cycle is the following: test plan, test scripts, document user acceptance documents etc. In the realization

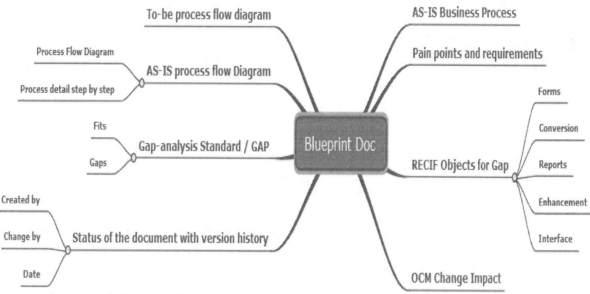

phase, activities are involved around following deliverables.

- System Configuration and configuration
- Testing Scenarios
- Functional Unit testing (FUT)
- Technical Unit Testing
- System Architecture
- Data Migration Documents

Go-live Preparation and Go-live

In the go-live phase, system readiness is tested. In the go-live preparation, data migration is tested in segments of mock tests. Then data readiness and system readiness tested. In the Go-live phase business process monitoring is one of key activity.

The deliverables and activities involved for Go-Live Preparation phase are the following:

- Fall back Plan
- Data Cleansing and finalization
- Data Migration Mock tests

In Go-live phase, the deliverables and activities are issue tracking, system handover document, end-user support, and planning for long-term support.

Best Practices:

SAP provides industry standards called "Best Practices". What is best practice? Best practice is the industry standard used by the industry. Best practice has given the industry highest value after international standards of ISO 9000. SAP process and function are based on best practice.

"Z" and "Y" customization:

The customization in SAP are saved with name or number. SAP recommends customization to start with "Z" and "Y", so it will not be over written in process of upgrade. By customization objects saved with "z" or "y" will not be overwritten in the upgrade process.

Summary Chapter 1

Chapter 1 Covered Topic:

SAP introduction with related topics and brief information about SAP ERP.

Basic terms and Conditions:

Introduction to Information technology related terms and more related to SAP ERP related terms with descriptions on subjects. Basics are essential to learn to learn any subject that why basics are covered in first chapter.

Notes

CHAPTER 2

ENTERPRISE STRUCTURE

CHAPTER 2: Summary

Enterprise structure

Brief overview of SAP Sales and Distribution enterprise structure setup and configuration steps.

Enterprise Structure:

- Enterprise Structure introduction
- Company
- Company Code
- Credit Control Area
- Sales Organization
- Distribution Channel
- Division
- Sales Area
- Sales Office
- Sales Group
- Plant
- Shipping Point
- Shipping Point Determination
- Business Area
- Visual Validation of Business Area
- Tips

Enterprise structure:

Business structure is the representation of a company and organizational element in system. Enterprise structure has different organizational elements separated by SAP ERP module wise. Each module in SAP has separate or integrated organizational business sections areas. The enterprise structure setup requires SME to analyze and design so transactional master data functions are utilized with optimum use of the system throughout planning that can save time and efforts in future.

The SAP system is integrated, so all enterprise structure elements connect or integrate on the highest level. In SAP, enterprise structure starts from company, then company code and under one company there could be multiple company codes. A company code is a representation of legal entity, and it has its set of elements unique to the company code. Each company code has a sales organization attached to it and sales organization has distribution channel and division under it, as we can see in the figure. The client is the logical database.

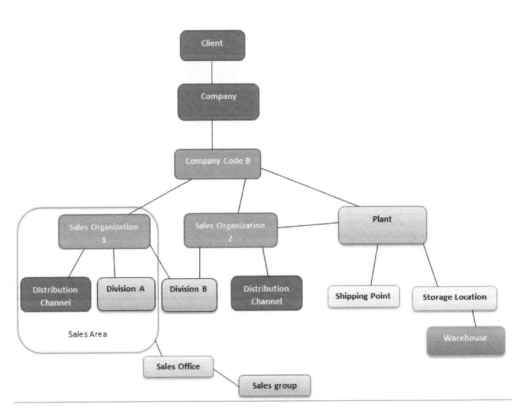

Tips: Most companies overlook on the importance of the well thought of design of enterprise structure and decide based on prospection and inexperience. Enterprise structure should be decided based on consideration of master data, transactional data, and complex process considerations. Most companies overlook enterprise structure setup which is foundation of SAP ERP system. If the enterprise structure is setup wrong, it means additional cost to the maintenance for the system in the long run.

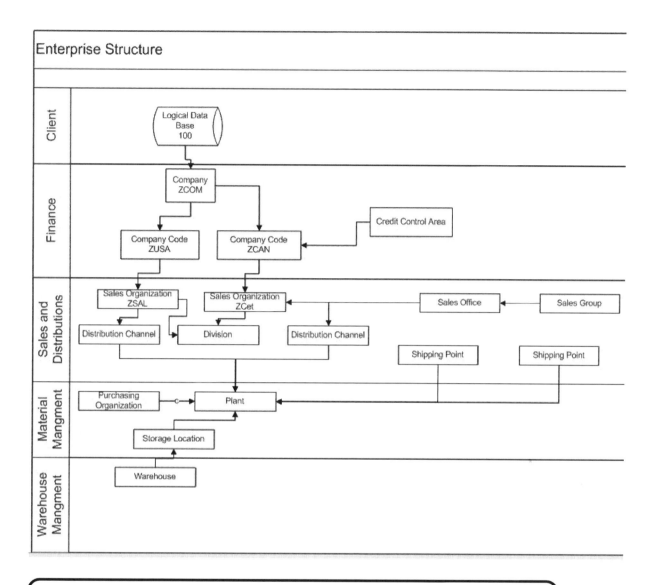

Enterprise Structure

```
Client

Finance

Sales and Distributions

Material Mangment

Warehouse Mangment
```

Enterprise structure is the way to represent origination structure in SAP

Implementation Guide Customization:

IMG refers to implementation guide customization. It also called back end customization. The end user does not have access to IMG or T-code because customization done by the subject matter expert. Implementation Guide referred as IMG customization.

Easy access menu path:

SAP Menus → Tools → Customizing → IMG → Execute Project

T-code for the same path is: **SPRO**

Client:

The client is logical database to create multiple systems on the same machine (server). The client is a logical system (logical database). The client number is required to be entered for SAP GUI log-in. Some customizations are specific to the client and some customizations are not client specific. The customizations that are global in nature can affect all the clients should be done with caution because change in development means it automatically will be in production, too. The client is single logical instances of the database.

Company:

The company represents a business, legal entity. One company can have multiple company codes assigned to it. In the system, the company can be represented by alpha or numeric values for the company representation. Company customization is a responsibility of SAP finance team and FICO consultant.

Example: Company "XYZ" can have one company code from United States and one company code from Canada. Each company code will be the legal entity formed in that country and has separate transactions specific to that company's code.

To create Company use T-code: **OX15**

IMG → Enterprise Structure → Definition → Financial Accounting → Define Company

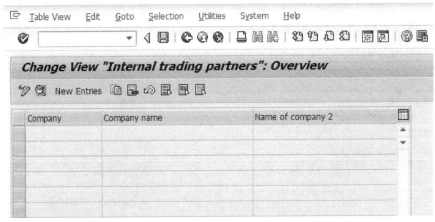

In the above screenshot, Company is defined with four characters. The company number can be alpha or numeric. In the second field for company name is and the third field is for company name 2.

Company Code:

Company code represents the financial, organizational unit. Company code generally represent legal entity under the same company. Company code customization done by FICO consultant. The company code based on legal entity representation. Company code has address, currency and language.

IMG → Enterprise Structure → Definition → Financial Accounting → Define Company code
Code use T-code. **OX02**

Credit Control Area:

Credit control area defines how customer credit should be setup in the system for credit related transactions. Control area customization can be independently or centrally managed. Credit control area controls the customer's credit functionality. The credit control area should have the same currency as company code. Each company code has one credit control assigned to it, but credit control can have many company codes assigned to it. The credit control area also can be assigned to multiple company codes. The credit control area is used in customer credit master creation. Credit Control Area customization is in the responsibility of SAP FI and SD modules area.

Credit Control Area Customization:

The credit control area can be set up: T-code OB45
IMG → Enterprise Structure → Definition → Financial Accounting → Define Credit Control Area

New Entries: Details of Added Entries

Cred.contr.area	
Currency	

Data for updating SD

Update	
FY Variant	

Default data for automatically creating new customers

Risk category	
Credit limit	
Rep. group	

Organizational data

☐ All co. codes

Credit control area:

The credit control area is four characters long and it could be alphanumeric combination.

Currency:

The currency must be same as company code currency.

Data for updating SD:

In these controls two elements which are relevant for sales and distribution related controls.

- **Update**
- **FY Variant**

Update:

This control uses of credit exposure sure of open sales documents, open deliver documents and open invoice document to be calculated in the credit process. Three different standard values can be used.

- **000012**
- **000015**
- **000018**
- **000012**

It looks at sales order lines with a confirmed delivery date. For delivery and billing it considers open delivery and billing document line value and include in the credit calculation. For new orders and transaction processing credit gets updated.

000015

For credit exposure for this selection considers the open delivery value and open billing value. For clearing account for it consider an unclear item for credit processing.

000018

This selection criteria for service related sales order when deliveries should not be considered. This credit exposure considers sales order, billing and financial open entries for credit processing.

FY Variant

This is used to set the fiscal year period for the credit control area.

Group is not copied to sales order and used to release by the control group representative.

All Company Codes:
The credit control area can be activated for all company codes in which credit control area has been defined and allowed for postings.

Assigning credit Control area to Company Code:

To assign a credit control area to company code use **T-code OB38**. Also for manual path from SPRO is
IMG → Enterprise Structure → Assignment → Financial Accounting →Assign company code to credit control area. (Select defines)
Company codes have an option to enter one credit control area to it, and with the option selected over write in the processing of transactions, credit control area can be changed and it will overwrite the old credit control area.

Sales Organization:

The sales organization is an organizational unit responsible for sales activity. This organizational element is represented in SAP by enterprise element. Sales organization defined in SAP alphabets or four numbers. Sales organization only assigned to one company code. One

Company code can have multiple sales organizations assigned to it. Sales organization can be defined based on location or business requirements. Sales organization customization come under the Sales and Distribution consultant.

T-code: **OVX5**

IMG → Enterprise Structure → Definition →Sales and Distribution → Define Sales Organization.

Sales Organization Business Tip:

Each sales area will generate additional master data if a customer is created in it. To save system resources, performance, database, complexity and efficiency, it is better to create less sales areas and used alternative fields for the grouping or functions of customers if possible.

⋆ Short Definition: Organizational unite that is responsible for sales.

Distribution Channel:

Distribution channels represent different ways of distribution of goods. Some examples of the distribution channel are: direct sales, online, retail, wholesale, etc. Distribution channel can be assigned to multiple sales organizations. Also sales and distribution channel also assigned to Plant.

Code use T-code: **OVXI**

IMG → Enterprise Structure → Definition →Sales and Distribution → Define Distribution Channel

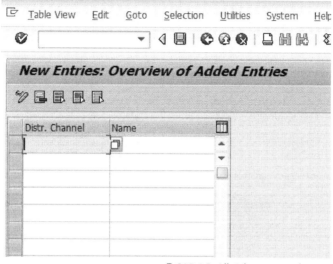

★ Short Definition: How products getting distributed.

Division:

The division represents "line of products". For example, company XYZ can have two different product lines, so they can be separated by different divisions. In SAP, division assigned to sales organization. Division can be assigned to multiple sales organizations, or used in the sales area setup.

Code use T-code: **OVXB**

IMG → Enterprise Structure → Definition →Logistics - General → Define Division

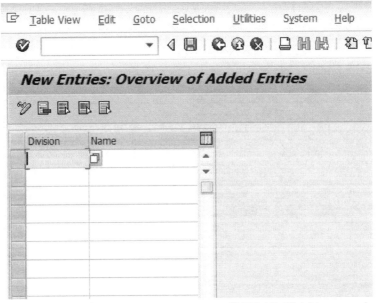

⋆ Short Definition: Line of Products

Sales Area:

Sales area is a unique combination of sales organization, distribution, and division. Sales area is used for master data setup and also becomes the basis for the transactions and master data creation. Sales area is required for customer master creation. In the sales area setup sales organization is assigned with distribution channel and division with unique combinations. Sales Area customization is configure by Sales and Distribution consultant or analyst.

Very Important ▪▪▪▪

Code use T-code: **OVXG**

IMG → Enterprise Structure → Assign →Setup Sales Area

Sales Org	Distribution	Division
1200	12	92
1200	14	10

Sales area for this example will be 1200 | 12 | 92 will be considered one sales area.

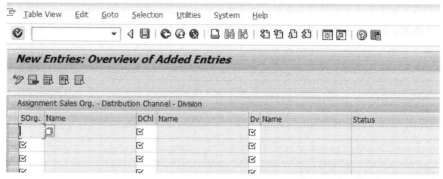

Sales Office:

A sales office is a business units in the sales department. Sales office is enterprise element used for sales activities and it is optional to use. In SAP Sales office can be useful to assign employees to specific sales office, sales order item level responsibility, sales document to the sales office, selection criteria for delivering and billing due list. Sales office has address property to the main office address. Sales office customization come under sales and distribution consultant.

T-code: **OVX1**
IMG → Enterprise Structure → Definition →Logistics → Define Sales Organization → Define Sales Office

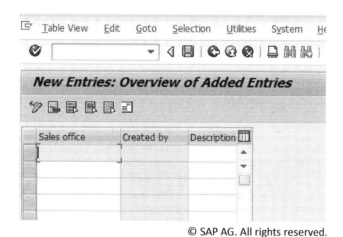

Sales Group:

SAP "sales group" represents the grouping of sales persons. Sales group is for assigning employee to the diverse groups for reporting of business functions. Sales group can be assigned to one sales office of multiple offices. This is one of the way to organize different sales groups.

Sales group can be useful in reporting, sales document item responsibility, and billing due list.

IMG → Enterprise Structure → Definition →Logistics → Define Sales Organization → Define Group
T-code: OVX4

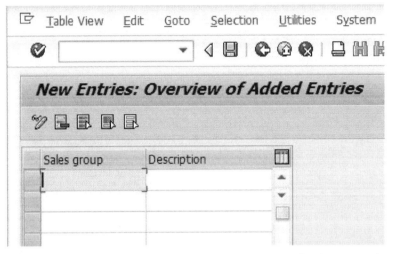

Plant:

Very Important

The plant is a representation of the factory or warehouse in SAP. The plant is assigned to one company code only, company code could have multiple plants assigned to it. The plant has shipping points assigned to it. A shipping point is a SAP organizational element under logistics. The plant has an address, language, and country. The plant is used for production, procurement, stock, and materials planning. Plant has finance implication.

- The plant has an address.
- The plant can only be assigned to one company code.
- A company can have many plant assigned to it.

T-code: OX10
IMG → Enterprise Structure → Definition →Logistics → Define Sales
Organization → Define Plant

Change View "Plants": Details

New Entries

Plant	0786
Name 1	ABC Company Inc.
Name 2	

Detailed information

Language Key	EN	English
House number/street	110 Main STEER	
PO Box	123	
Postal Code	62226	
City	Belliville	
Country Key	US	United States
Region	IL	New York
County code	US	County in NY
City code		
Tax Jurisdiction		
Factory calendar		

Note: The address fields Name1 and Name2 are not copied from the address
         screen and you must maintain them separately.
         All other addr. data can only be maintained in addr. screen.
         The changes can only be seen in the overview and detail view
         after they have been saved.

Shipping Point:

Shipping point is the location where goods are shipped or received from. The plant has multiple shipping and receiving points assign to it. Shipping points are SAP enterprise element that require customization. Shipping point is assigned to the Plant. Shipping point can be assigned to multiple plants. One shipping point has multiple loading points if needed. Delivery always process from shipping point. Shipping point has its own address. Shipping point gets to determine in the sales order. Each plant has at least one shipping point.

T-code: **OVXD**
IMG → Enterprise Structure → Definition →Logistics → Logistic Execution → Define Shipping Point

A shipping point factory calender defines the holiday and work days as per factory calender. Woking hours can be configured in shipping point as well. Time can be configured for loading, picking, and routing work day.

Change View "Shipping Points": Details

New Entries

Shipping Point	0564	Shipping Point - DOC1

Location

Country	IN	Departure Zone	

Times

Factory Calendar	
Working Times	

Determine Times

Determine Load. Time	No loading time determination
Det.Pick/Pack Time	Pick/pack time not determined
Rounding Work Days	

Form Text Names

Address Text Name	
Letter Header Text	
Text Name Foot.Lines	
Text Name Greeting	
Text Name SDB Sender	

Print Picking List

Output Type	
Message Language	
Number of Messages	
Send Time	
Transmission Medium	
Subsystem	

Background Processing

Displ.info

Others

Pick confirmation

Business Area:

The business area is used for monitoring section of the business for internal use for reporting and monitoring. Business area comes under Financial accounting configuration with FI-SD integration. It integrates with finance module for reporting purposes.

T-code: OX03

IMG → Enterprise Structure → Definition →Financial Accounting → Define Business Area

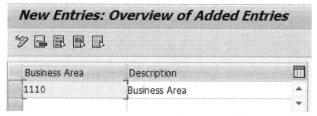

Business Area Assignment:

The business area is determined by the rules that are assigned to it. Business area is assigned to the plant and division. Business area also has an option to be assigned to the sales area.

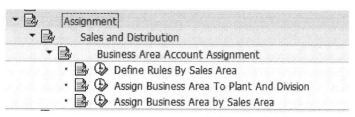

Business Area determination:

Business determination based on three rules:

- Plant and Item division
- Sales area
- Sales Organization, distribution channel and item division

Business Area Determine Plant and Item Division:

Business area determines by the plant and item division is under sales and distribution, but also integrate with finance on the definition of business area.

T-code: OVF0

IMG → Enterprise Structure → Assignment → Sales and Distribution → Business Area Account Assignment → Assign Business Area to Plant and Division

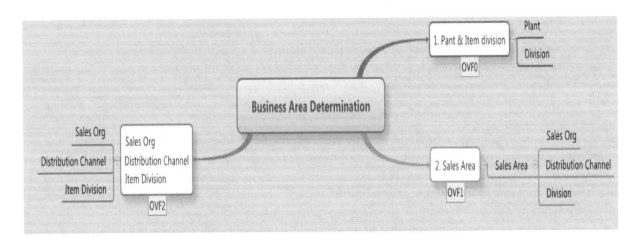

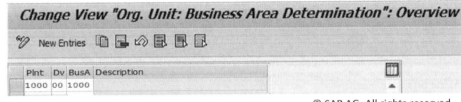

Business Area Determine by Sales Area:

A business area determination based on sales in area.

T-code: OVF0

IMG → Enterprise Structure → Assignment → Sales and Distribution → Business Area Account Assignment → Assign Business Area to sales area

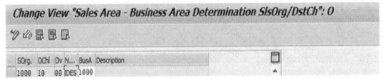

Based on the sales area in transaction business is will be determined accordingly.

Business Area Determine by Sales Organization, distribution channel and item division:

T-code: OVF2

IMG → Enterprise Structure → Assignment → Sales and Distribution → Business Area Account Assignment → Define Rule by Sales Area

Rules are set, how business should be derived, and based on this setting business area will be determined. Three rules the third rule is sales organization, distribution and division.

Validation Of enterprise Structure:

After the enterprise structure configuration setup, it needs to be verified. One of the ways to validate enterprise structure in SAP is to view assignments in configuration. The assignment also shows on graphically with T-code: **EC01**

First select Structure ![Structure] [1] then select Navigation ![Navigation] [2] and from the list of company code double click on the company code where enterprise structure configuration has been done. Then select company code and double click on it and view all the assignments.

Tips:

- SAP best practice is very good source to implement effective enterprise structure.
- SAP Building Blocks also is another good source information.

---

[1]

[2]

Chapter 2 Summary

Enterprise structure is a very important step for the SAP ERP software setup. Enterprise structure define functionality of the system. Enterprise structure should be analyzed with expert consideration. Well though enterprise structure can improve lot of business process and leverage best practices by the industry.

The following are important Enterprise structure elements configuration is been setup.

- Company
- Company Code
- Credit Control area
- Sales organization
- Distribution channel
- Division
- Sales Area
- Sales Group
- Plant
- Shipping Point
- Business Area

Exercise on Enterprise structure:

1. How many company code one plant be assigned to?
2. How many Plants one company code have?
3. Can credit control area assigned to multiple company codes?
4. How sales area setup effect on master data?
5. What is sales line?
6. How to validate Enterprise structure?
7. In which module plant and the Division is defined?
8. Can sales organization can be assigned to multiple company codes?

Answers:

8) Sales organization only can be assigned to one company code to track sales related to the company code.

7) Plant and Division belong to the Logistic general module area.

6) To validate enterprise structure, check the links in EC01 graphically. Also on the enterprise structure in most places SAP provide a check, copy, and edit enterprise objects it can be checked this way too.

5) Combination of sales organization and distribution called sales line.

4) Sales are increase master data record and system complexity when same customer is extended too many sales areas. The sales area can be used if it required but software development and team can achieve system efficiency performance by many other ways to maintain functionality. For example, customer group, customer industry, listing and exclusion, pricing, and much more.

3) Credit control can be assigned to multiple company codes and also each company code also can have different credit control areas assigned to it, credit management.

2) Company code can have many plant assigned to it.

1) Plant only can be assigned to one company code.

Notes

CHAPTER 3

MASTER DATA

Topics of Master Data Chapter:

- Master Data
- Transactional Data
- Customer Master
- Common Division and Distribution channel
- Account Group Customization
- Customer Partner Function Customization
- Vendor Master SAP MM
- Material Master
- Material Type
- Customer Master Info Records
- Payment Terms
- Payment Plan Customization
- Table View topics
- Table View Old (SE16)
- Table View New (SE16N)

Master Data:

Very Important ▪▪▋█

Master data hardly changes. Master data is the means of transactions, for example, customer, and products (material) considered master data. Master Data is required to create sales orders, delivery, invoice, etc. SAP Sales and Distribution master data elements are customer Master, Material Master, and Pricing Records. The master data are based on group of tables for each master data. To represent one master data, each table represents a unique view of the master data. In SAP Sales and Distribution Customer master, material master and condition records are important master data.

In Sales and distribution few of master data examples that are relevant to sales order processing in general.

- Customer Master Data
- Material Master Data
- Pricing Condition Records
- Customer material Info Record

Transactional Data:

Transactional data is dynamic in nature; it changes transaction to transaction. The constant changes of sales order represent transactional data because. Like inquiry, sales orders, delivery, and billing documents all are example of transnational data.

> ★ Short Definition: ★
> Transactional data is dynamic in nature
> Transactional data changes more frequently.

Customer Master Data:

Customer master represents customer information in a system and many functionalities from customer master field values. Customer master defines and uses different business functions with different roles for the controls. Customer master is divided into three different views.

> # Data that rarely change and the means of transections

Customer Master Data is saved with three different views:

1. **General Data**
2. **Company Code Data**
3. **Sales Area Data**

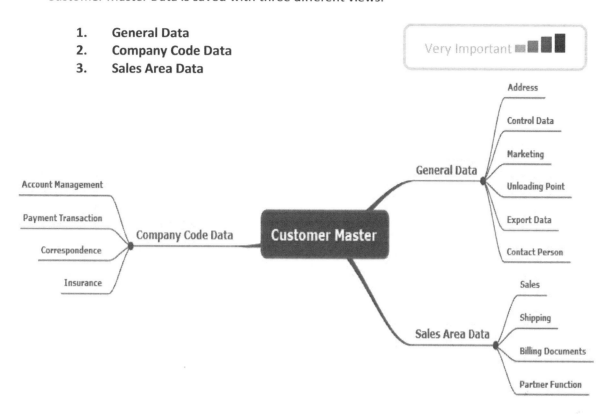

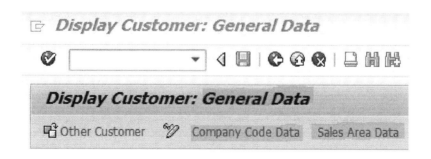

Customer Master has three views.

Master data is required for transactional data.

Three different views are created to maintain different business sections. This view also relates to functions, or roles. Customer Master can be created with two combinations: General data with Company code and data or General data with Sales area Data. The Customer Master also can be maintained centrally with all the views. In General Data, it consists of general information like: name, address, P.O box address, and phone number, fax number, and so on. Sales Data consist of billing, shipping, pricing, related information, and partner functions. With master data in Customer Master, additional data also available for control, and functionality.

General Data

The General data consists of name, address, phone, and fax from the address tab. With Each tab from the Customer Master General Data has more detail information from customer Master. To view customer T-code is used XD01

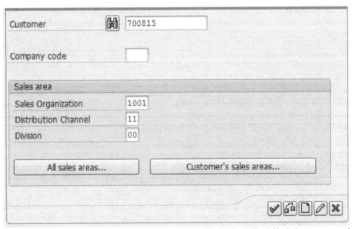

To view user should enter: customer number, company code, and sales area number.

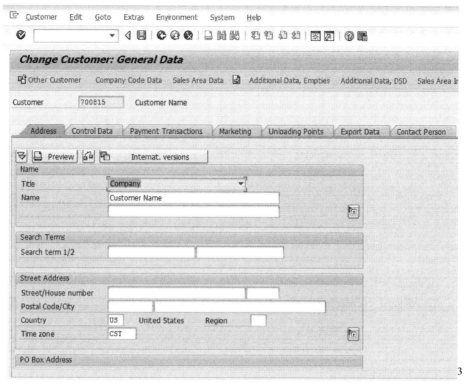

Each view has heading on top of the page to represent each view

---

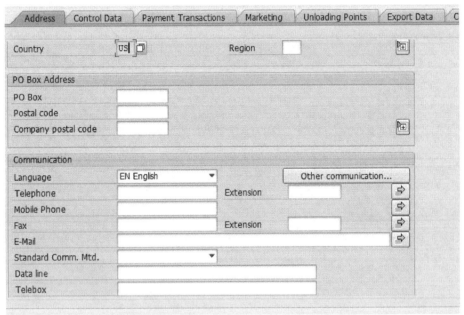

2. Company Code Data

Company code data have customer financial related information. The additional information can be seen in the screenshot.

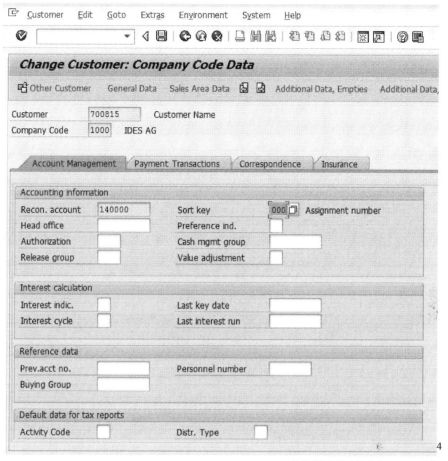

3. Sales Data

Sales area consist of a unique combination of sales organization, distribution channel, and division. Sales data also has additional information related to that sales area like plant, partner function, shipping and billing information.

To create a customer master three different T-codes are followed.

1. XD01   Centrally with all the views
2. FD01   General and Company code Data
3. VD01   General and Sales Data

XD01 include all the views to be maintained. VD01 include sales area and general area views and FD01 only for company code view with general data to be maintained.

In sales or view of customer master four tabs are following.

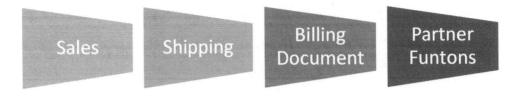

Sales Area Data each tab has many fields.

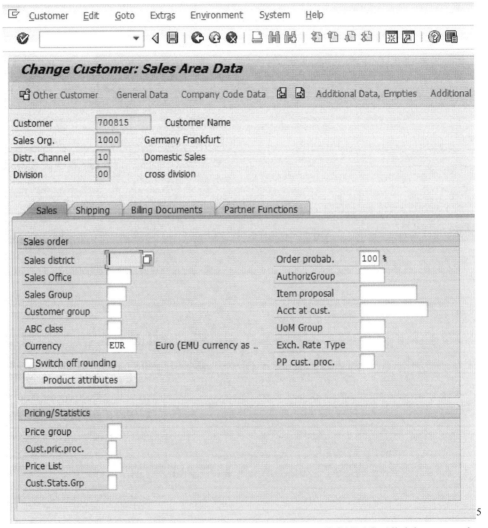

Customer Master Partner Functions:

Partner function is the role of customer in the transaction. For example, customers can have many shipping address so this customer has many ships to partner functions. In general mainly Customer Master has four partner functions. They sold to customer never change only ship to, bill to and payer change in customer master.

1. Sold to Party
2. Ship to Party
3. Bill to Party
4. Payer

Additional partner functions can be added to the customer master. There can be multiple "bills to" and multiple payer function can be added for one customer. For each customer the "Sold to" partner function can be created once only.

Additional Partner Functions:

The following are few of the additional partner functions that can be configured and assigned to the customer master.

- Freight forwarder
- Sales representative
- Contact person
- Sales representative

Customer Master Related T-codes:

NO	Description	T-code
1	Create Customer Master (Centrally)	XD01
2	Change Customer Master (Centrally)	XD02
3	Display Customer Master (Centrally)	XD03
4	Create Customer Master with Company code View	FD01
5	Change Customer Master with Company code View	FD02
6	Display Customer Master with Company code View	FD03
7	Create Customer Master Sales View	VD01
8	Change Customer Master Sales View	VD02
9	Display Customer Master Sales View	VD03
10	Block Customers	VD05
11	Delete Customer	VD06
12	Display Change's	VD04
13	Mass update	XD99
14	Create Contact Person	VAP1

Centrally mean all the view of the customer Master with single t-code.

Mass update allows multiple customer change at once.

Display changes show when the customer master was changed and by which user.

Customer Master Related Tables:

The following are some of the customer Master tables.

Table	Description
KNA1	General Data
KNB1	Company Code Data
KNVV	Customer Sales Data
KNAT	Customer Master Tax Grouping
KNBK	Customer Master Back Detail
KNB5	Customer Master Dunning Data
KNKK	Customer Credit Management Data
KNMT	Customer Material Info Record Data
KNVI	Customer Master Tax Indicator
KNVP	Customer Master Partner Function

To view table use T-code SE16N or SE16

Create Customer Master centrally (XD01) means, all required views of customer are maintained at same time. Create Customer Master with finance View (FD01) means two views are maintained General Data and Company code data. Create customer Master with Sales view means two view of customer aster is maintained Sales view and General data.

Contact Person partner function:

Master data is used as a business partner's function in customer master. It can be created separately or entered into while creating or changing customer.

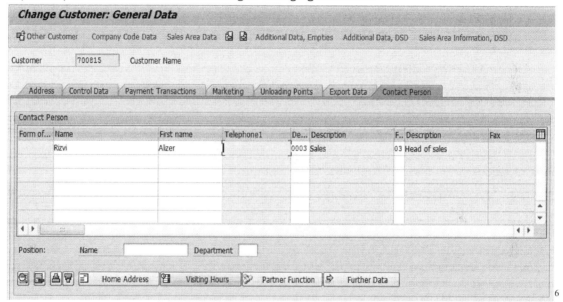

T-code for Contact person is: **VAP1**

Customer Master Customization:

The first step for customization for customer master is for account group. After account group partner functions are configured.

Account Group Customization:

Account group controls followings:

- **Customer Number range**
- **Field status of Customer Master**
- **Partner Determination**

Define Customer Number range:

The number range is used to define customer number. The number range can be internal number or external number range. In internal number range the customer number will be picked by the system and with external number the customer number can be manually entered at the time of customer creation. Number range can be included in transport otherwise it is a manual activity to perform in system landscape setup.

Customization Path from SPRO T-code is

IMG →Financial Accounting → Account receivable and Account Payable → Customer Account → Master Data → Define Number Range for customer Account Group

T-code for customization: **XDN1**

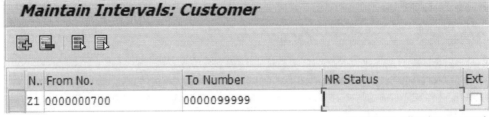

Maintain Intervals: Customer

N..	From No.	To Number	NR Status	Ext
Z1	0000000700	0000099999		☐

Number range: it is two letter field is used to assign to account group and based on this number range customer number are generated.

Define Account Group:

Customization Path from SPRO t-code is

IMG →Financial Accounting → Account receivable and Account Payable → Customer Account → Master Data → Define Account Group

T-code for customization: **OBD2**

Change View "Customer Account Groups": Details

Edit field status   New entries   📋 🗑 ◀ ▶ 🖨   BC Set: Field Value Origin

Account group   0001

General data

Meaning	Sold-to party
One-time account	☐
Output determ.proc.	

Field status

General data

Company code data

Sales data

Field Status Group:

Field status group controls the status of the field in customer master. Field status communicates the status of field in the transaction or master data. Four field statuses used: mandatory, hidden, display, and optional. The field status group can be controlled by account group. Account group controls the each field status by configuration setup.

- Suppress
- Required Entry
- Optional Entry
- Display

The field status group applied to the each tab level of customer Master.

Maintain Field Status Group: Address

📄 Field check

| General Data | | | | | Page 1 / 2 |

Acct group   0001
Sold-to party
General data

Address

	Suppress	Req. Entry	Opt. entry	Display
Name 1/last name	○	●	○	○
Form of address	○	○	●	○
Search term A	○	○	●	○
Name 2/first name	○	○	●	○
Name 3, name 4	○	○	●	○
Postal code, city	○	○	●	○
Street	○	○	●	○
District	○	○	●	○
Region	○	●	○	○

In the above screenshot is from the customer master address tab. The first field "Name /last name"
The above screenshot is from the customer master address tab. The first field "Name /last name"
made required field so based on this customization; this field will be required at the time of
customer creation.

Account group screenshot.

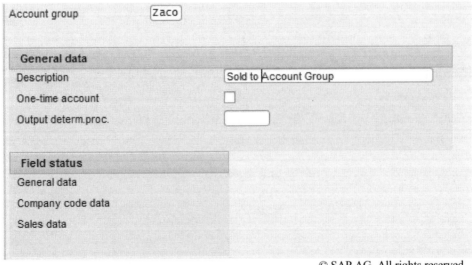

Account group   Zaco

General data

Description	Sold to Account Group
One-time account	☐
Output determ.proc.	

Field status

General data
Company code data
Sales data

Account group controls, customer number, field's setup and partner function.

One Time Customer:

One time customer only used once so it can be selected here in this customization. If account group need to be made for a one time customer then the one time customer check box need to be checked.

Output Determination Procedure:

This field is used for type of output determination. An output procedure used to define what output can be determined from the account group. Generally this field is not used in most cases.

Customer Partner Function Determination:

Partner function defines the customer role with many transactions. Each customer could have multiple partner functions. The main four partner functions are following:

- Sold To
- Ship To
- Bill to
- Payer

Additional partner functions, customizable.

- Contact Person
- Sales Manager

The partner functions can be configured as they are required. The partner function determination can be configured for following transactions.

Partner Function determination at transaction level is the following:

- Partner Function Determination
- Sales order header level
- Sales order item level
- Delivery Item Level
- Delivery Header
- Shipment
- Billing Header Level
- Billing item level
- Partner Function at sales activity

All of transaction configurations are same, so the partner function customization will be focused on standard partner function determination and it is almost same as for all of the above.

Customization Path from SPRO T-code is

IMG →Sales and Distribution → Basic Functions → Set Up Partner Determination

Steps for partner function determination are following:

Partner Functions → Partner Determination Procedure → Asign Partner Function in procedure → Partner Determination Proceure Assinment → Acccount Grp Functional Asingment

Here is screenshot of partner function determination customization steps.

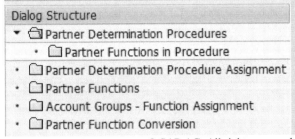

Partner Functions:

For the customization we will be focusing on standard partner functions.

- Sold To
- Ship To
- Bill To
- Payer

In this step we define partner functions with two letter abbreviated identification.

Part...	Name	Part...	Error ...	Sup...	U...	CHT...
SP	Sold-to Party	KU	07		☑	
BP	Bill-to Party	KU	07		☐	
PY	Payer	KU	07		☐	
CR	Carrier	LI	08		☐	
TF	Freight service agt	LI	08		☐	
SH	Ship-to Party	KU	07		☐	

The partner Function field is the two characters long name of the partner function. The name field description of the partner function needs to be maintained. Partner function type is the type of partner function; the following are a few examples of the partner function type.

Partner Function Type	Description
KU	Customer
AP	Contact Person
LI	Vendor
US	User

The partner function type defines what kind of partner function it is. If the partner function is vendor then it means we pay the vendor for service or product vendor provides.

Error group is an incompletion procedure and it will auto populate. A superior Partner function is used to setup customer high level partner function. Unique field used to define the uniqueness of partner function. For example: hierarchy partner function and sold should be unique field so this function should not repeat in customer master. Field "CH Type" representing customer hierarchy type, it is used to define what type of customer hierarchy is used.

Partner Determination Procedure:

Partner Determination Procedures	
Part.Det.Proc	Name
ZACT	Test Procedure

In this step we define the partner function procedure. The Procedure could be two to four letter characters with description of the procedure. The procedure is used for Partner Functions assignment. The partner functions which are defined previously will be assigned into the procedure. We can make partner function non modifiable and also make the partner function mandatory with customization.

Partner Determination Procedure Assignment:

Partner Functions in Procedure					
Part...	Partn...	Name	Not Modifia...	Mandat.Funct	
ZACT	PY	Payer	☐	☐	▲
ZACT	SP	Sold-to-Party	☐	☐	
ZACT	SH	Ship-to party	☐	☐	
ZACT	BB	Bill to party	☐	☐	

In the above screenshot ZACT is Procedure next field is partner function.

In this step the account group gets assigned to the partner determination procedure. This configuration allows procedure partner function into the account group.

Accountancy Group - Function Assignment:

Account Groups - Function Assignment				
Partn.Funct.	Name	Account Grp	Name	
SH		0001		▲

In this configuration step all the partner function is assigned to the account group individually.

Partner Function Conversion:

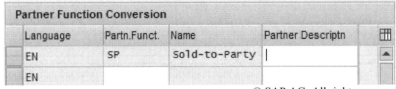

Partner Function Conversion				
Language	Partn.Funct.	Name	Partner Descriptn	
EN	SP	Sold-to-Party		▲
EN				

This customization controls the language of customer master partner function.

Common Distribution Channel:

Common distribution channel is customization in sales and distribution for defining common distribution channel for master data. Based on this the sales org can be come under common distribution channel instead of extending sales are to multiple distribution channel. It also called referenced condition because the master data distribution channel is conditional record or grouping.

Customization T-Code: VOR1

IMG → Sales and Distribution → Master Data → Define Common Distribution Chanel

Common Division:

Common Division is used when grouping of division is required in the sales area into single common division. Common division streamlines the master data maintenance and common sales are can be maintained from this function into common conditional master data for sales area use.

Customization T-Code: VOR2

IMG → Sales and Distribution → Master Data → Define Common Division

Vendor Master SAP MM:

Vendor master is the supplier or service provider for the purchasing department. Vendor Master has three views similar to the Customer Master. Vendor master also requires configuration of the partner determination account group, but vendor master belongs to a material management module and it is procurement related activities.

- General Data
- Company Code Data
- Purchasing Organization View

Moderately Important ▪▪▪▪▪

General Data has fields including name, address, phone number, phone number, fax, P.O Box, etc.

Purchasing Organization has the fields of partner functions, purchasing, group pricing indicator, etc.

The company Code view has financial related information such as reconciliation account number, industry sector, etc.

T-code to create vendor XK01

Change Vendor: Initial Screen

Menu ▲ | ◀ Back Exit Cancel System ▲ | Select all Deselect all

Vendor [   ] 🗖
Company Code [   ]
Purch. Organization [   ]

General data
☐ Address
☐ Control
☐ Payment transactions
☐ Contact Persons

Company code data
☐ Accounting info
☐ Payment transactions
☐ Correspondence
☐ Withholding tax

Purchasing organization data
☐ Purchasing data
☐ Partner functions

Material Master:

Material master is a representation of product information. Product or material is used for sale, raw material, services material, and finished products. SAP Martial Master has detailed master data information with multiple views. Material Master has detailed information about product specification divided in different views. These views belong to different modules like Material management's procurement views, sales, and distribution's sales views, and general views. Each module has relevant master data controls and functions. Material master views configured for Material Type.

Sales side of material master views are following:

Basic Data 1
Basic Data 2
Sales Org. 1
Sales Org. 2
General / Plant Data
Foreign Trade: Export Data

Important Topic ▄▄█▉

Sales Text
Accounting 1
Accounting 2

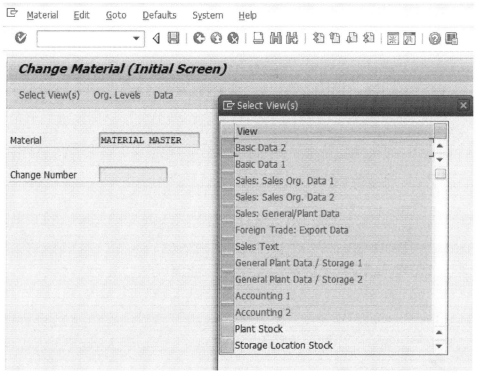

Material Type:

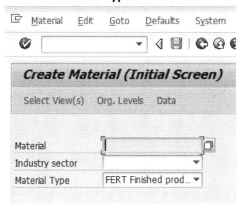

Material Type categorizes different between types of Materials. It controls material views and field status. New material type can be customized for the field status group. Here are few examples of material types.

Material Type	Description
FERT	Finish product:
HAWA	Trading good:
NLAG	Non-stock material
RAW	Raw material
VERP	Packaging material
DIEN	Services (non-stock items)

Industry sector:

Industry sector defines what kind of industry is assigned to the material master.

Material Master T-codes:

The following are some of the transaction codes for material master.

Transaction Code	Description
MM01	Creating Material Master
MM02	Change Material Master
MM03	View Material Master
MM12	Material Master Change on schedule
MM06	Flag for deletion
MM17	Mass maintenance
MMAM	Change Material Type
MMBE	Stock overview
MMPV	Close Period

The following are some of the tables for Materiel Master.

Table Name	Description
MARA	General Material Data
MARC	Plant Data for Material
MVKE	Sales Data for Material
MAKT	Material Master Description
MBEW	Material valuation (accounting)
MLAN	Tax classification
T179	Product Hierarchies
STXH	STXD SAPscript text file header
STXL	STXD SAPscript text file lines

Material Type:

Material Type can be customized for views that allowed for the material and field status group. Material type configuration is not belonged to general logistics. The scope of this topic is covered limited for better understanding how the material type controls material master related filed and functions.

T-code: **OMS2**

IMG → Logistics General → Material Master → Basic Setting → Material Types → Define Attribute of Material Types

The following areas are at Material Type controls:

- Special Material Type
- General data
- User Departments
- Internal and internal Purchase Order
- Classification
- Valuation
- Quantity / Value Updating
- Retail Specific fields

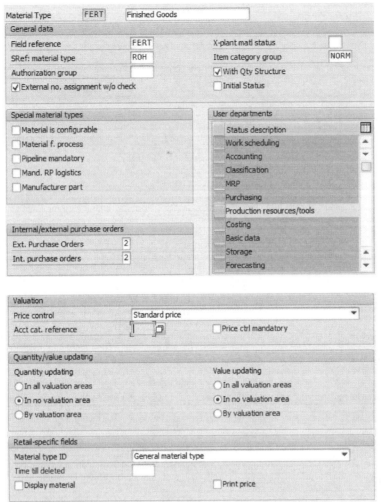

Customer Material Info Records

Customer material info record is master data. CMIR put preference in sales order creation over master data. For example, if a customer may have its own material amount of their purchase order, then in the sales document, then the system will substitute values from customer material info record into sales orders. Customer material info record also can override values from Unite of measure, Plant data, rounding profile, and delivery priority. These values are maintained in master data but preference come from the Customer material info record.

T-code to create a Customer material info record is the following:

Create: VD51
Change: VD52
Display: VD53

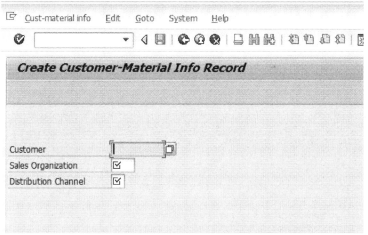

Customer Material info record can base on customer number + sales organization + Distribution channel.

Tables for CMIR is KNMT

Payment Terms:

The payment term defines the term of payments. Payment term used in transaction like sales order. If payment terms is net thirty, it means the net is due upon thirty discounts is offered for early payment. If payment is delayed, then the customer will be dunned and issued a letter based on the business process and procedure of the organization.

The payment term is used in sales documents and also can be assigned to the customer master so the customer specific payment term automatically come into sales order creation. The payment term can be changed in sale order creation and entered if not maintain for the customer master.

Payment term configuration marked for customer and vendor. Payment term also can have an installment plan assigned to it too.

Payt Terms	ZNET	Sales text	4 days 4%, 15 Day 1%, Net 30
Day limit		Own explanation	

Account type	Baseline date calculation
☑ Customer	Fixed day ☐
☑ Vendor	Additional months ☐

Pmnt block/pmnt method default	Default for baseline date
Block key ☐ ☐	⦿ No default ◯ Posting date
Payment Method ☐ ☐	◯ Document date ◯ Entry date

Payment terms

☐ Installment payment   ☐ Rec. Entries: Supplement fm Master

Term	Percentage	No. of days	/	Fixed date	Additional months
1.	4,000 %	4		☐	☐
2.	1,000 %	15		☐	☐
3.		30		☐	☐

Explanations

within 4 days 4 % cash discount	within 15 days 1 % cash discount
within 30 days Due net	

In the screenshot Payment term has discount four percent if dues are paid in four days, one percent discount if payment is received within fifteen days and total are due in thirty days. This payment term is without payment plan.

Configuration for Payment Term:

Implementation Guide path from SPRO

IMG → Financial Accounting → Account receivable account payable → Outgoing Invoice/Credit Memo → Maintain Term of Payment

T-code: OBB8

Payment Plan of Payment Term:

The payment plan is used in payment term with the payment installments. The installment equal out to the total invoice due and payment term need to be marked in the configuration for the installments and the system will carry out the payment term for each payment.

Configuration for Payment Term:

Implementation Guide path from SPRO

IMG → Financial Accounting → Account receivable account payable → Outgoing Invoice/Credit Memo → Define Terms of Payment for Installment Payment

T-code: OBB9

Terms of Paymen	Inst	Percent	Pmnt term
I20	1	50.000	A003
I20	2	50.000	A004
I30	1	33.333	A003
I30	2	33.333	A004
I30	3	33.334	A005

The terms of payment have installments define that how many installment this term of payment has and percentage and for each percentage is in payment term so the invoice can be divided into payment installment.

SAP SD Material Determination:

Material determination is product substitution of newer product or when the old product is outdated. The new product or similar products can be replaced or subtitle in the sales order. When a business offers newer model of product similar to the previous product, it can be automated with material determination configuration.

Example: black, blue-ray player can be replaced with a white, blue ray player; that is a simple example also last year model can be replace this year product also one more example of material determination. Material determination is used if the company comes up with a new model of phone and old phone becoming obsolete so that material determination can be used for parts are replaced by new ones. The same product with different packaging also can be replaced with material determination.

 The benefit of this functionality is that when business is out of material or product then instead of manually researching replaceable product, this process can streamline the sales process.

Customization:

The material determination configuration based on the principle of condition technique. After the configuration condition record needed to be created from material substituted for determining material in the sales order.

Maintain Table for Material Substitution:

Customization Path: from T-code SPRO
IMG → Sales and Distribution → Basic Functions → Material Determination → Maintain Prerequisites for Material determination (from the selection box select "Create Condition Tables").

T-code: OV16

Condition table is created for fields that material need being substituted. The standard tables are two in the system "001 material entered" and "002 sales area + material entered" The new table entry can be created as per requirements.

Maintain Access Sequence:

T-code SPRO

IMG → Sales and Distribution → Basic Functions → Material Determination → Maintain Prerequisites for Material determination (from the selection box select "Maintain Access Sequence").

Access sequence is a search limit with the table fields. In the access sequence, we enter tables.

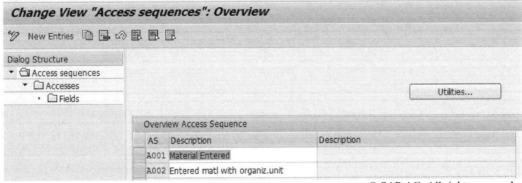

In access sequence A001 access it shows the table entry.

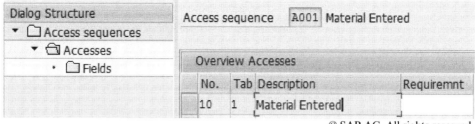

In the above screenshot it is displaying Accesses (as folder icon is open) in this field the "No" field represents the sequence number of access sequence, and fled "Tab" represent a table entry in access sequence.

Condition Type:

T-code SPRO

IMG → Sales and Distribution → Basic Functions → Material Determination → Maintain Prerequisites for Material determination (from the selection box select "Condition Type").

Condition type A001 would be assigned to access sequence A001 in screen shot. It also has validity function valid from and to dates.

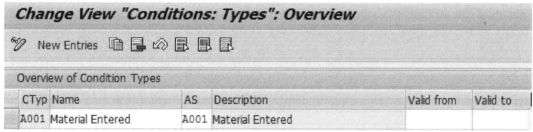

Material determination Procedure:

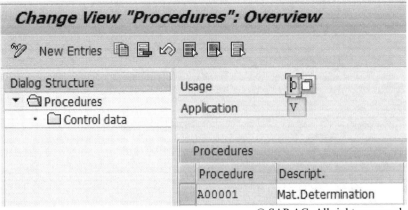

Material determination procedure is defined in the above screenshot and in the next step by selecting procedure going into Control data for further controls in procedure.

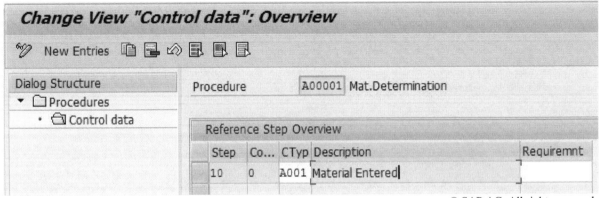

Material determination has four fields for customization.

- Step
- Counter
- Condition Type
- Requirement Type

Step: Step is the counter in material determination procedure. It is used to indicate system to which step should be processed first. The step start with 10 and the second step 20, so if additional steps require it can be added in-between.

Counter: Counter is used if same step is repeated and had additional process it can be added to count to process it in counter sequence.

Condition Type: Condition Type is customized in this field, the step and a counter field related to the condition type for the process of condition type.

Requirement Type: Requirement Type is a program which can be customized to process additional functions for material determination. The standard requirement type can be used, but additional requirement type customization requires ABAP development.

Material Substitution Reason:

Material substitution also can be customized based on the substitution reason.

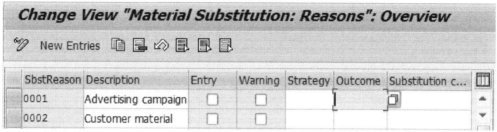

SbstReason	Description	Entry	Warning	Strategy	Outcome	Substitution c...	
0001	Advertising campaign	☐	☐		☐		
0002	Customer material	☐	☐				

Substitution Reason:

The automatic substitution reason the first field to configure for automatic substitution to be determines.

Entry:

Entry is the second control in substitution reason controls, if this option is selected the original entry will be printed. Based on requirement if original material needs to be printed or not this option can be used accordingly.

Warning:

Warning field is the third option in substitution reason controls. If this option is selected the system will issue warranting message before material substitution. This option can be used if warning message is needed for the user to be aware that new material is determined.

Strategy:

Strategy is fourth control in substitution reason customization. It controls if material need to be selected automatically in back ground or they require to be selected manually.

Outcome:

The Outcome is the fifth option for customization in substitution reason controls. This field value control if substitution should carry out or substitution items show in sub items or only relevant for sales order creation process with the option of showing in sub items.

Substitution Category:

Substitution Category is sixth customization in substitution reason controls. It controls service related functions to be controlled. The service item can be categorized for substitution.

Material Deamination Condition Record:

The mater determination condition record is master data. The T-code is used for the materiel determination is VB11.

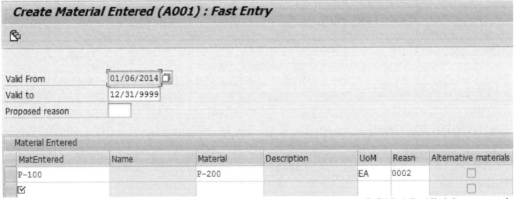

Validity from and Valid To:

The material determination has validity period controls.

Chapter 3 Summary:

Following topics covered in the chapter:

- Introduction to Master Data
- Transactional Data
- Customer Master Data and related topics
- Customer Master customization
- Account Group customization
- Partner Function Determination
- Introduction to Material Master
- Material Type Configuration
- Introduction to Customer Material information Record

Notes

CHAPTER 4

ORDER MANGMENT & CONTRACTS

Chapter 4: Order Management and Contract

Chapter 4: Topics

- Contracts
- Quantity Contracts
- Value Contract
- Service Contract
- Master Contract
- Scheduling Agreement
- Sales Order Customization
- Item Category Customization
- Item Category Determination
- Plant Determination
- Route determination Customization
- Dynamic Item Proposal Customization
- Schedule line customization
- Schedule Line determination
- Rebate Agreement
- Quantity Contract
- Sales Document Block
- Sales Order Customizing

> # Contract is legal agreement between buyer

Contract

A contract is a legal agreement. It is a written document and agreed upon binding document. The contract has validity date. It has term and conditions. Sales and Distribution have four types of contracts are available. Schedule agreement also considers type as a contract. The contract is one of the first steps, but not all sales process requires contracts. It depends on the requirement. In Sales and Distribution contract type customization and sales order customization is same.

Contract Types:

The following are four types of contracts.

1. Quantity Contract
2. Value Contract
3. Service Contract
4. Master Contract

Quantity Contract:

Quantity Contract is based on quantity. If quantity contract exists, it will issue a warning in the sales order. With customization as it also can have reference mandatory, so sales process will require quantity contract type reference mandatory. Example: Customer can be bound to buy 100 pieces per each sales order.

To create contract, the T-code is **VA41**
The quantity contract order type is used **QT**

Value Contract:

Value contract is based on value. Value contract calculates the value with an assortment or selected product. Two kinds of value contracts in system one with assortment and one with fix product. Unlike quantity contract, it depends on the value of the sales order. For example, if a customer places an order, regardless of quantity of material, the value should match contract value.

To create contract, the T-code is **VA41**
Value contract order type: **WK1**
Value contract order type: **WK2** (Material Related)

Contracts are presales activity document.

Service Contract:

Service contracts are a based on services Example customer create a service contract with a wireless company provider for one year of service.

To create contract, the T-code is: **VA41**
Service and Maintenance contract order type: **SC**

Master Contract:

Master contract is a combination of quantity contract, value, contract, and service contract. Example: if customer having multiple contracts they can be combined into one master contract. Master contract could only contain only two types of contracts, it does not require to have all three types of contract.

To create contract, the T-code is **VA41**
Master contract order type: **GK**

Scheduling Agreement:

Scheduling agreement is a type of a contract, but it functions like sales document. The scheduling agreement is created with periodic delivery schedule and billing is based on delivery of goods. If customers make a bulk order, but want recurring shipments periodically, then scheduling agreement can help the process. It helps with repeated orders or demand with a schedule of periodic deliveries.

To create Scheduling Agreement the T-code is: VA31
Order type: CO
Many other types of scheduling agreement available: LZ, CO, LZM and etc.

Scheduling agreement is a sales document that has periodic delivery scheduling.

Rebate Agreement:

The rebate is a type of a discount with accrual condition. When a customer buys a product and condition get fulfills then customer received a credit back. The only difference between regular discount and rebate is that the credit is given back to the customer after the purchase the sales order and discount give to the customer at the time of sales order or invoice.

Rebate condition can be based on customer purchase volume, product rebate or other basis. The first rebate agreement is setup, it will contain percentage or fix price, discount, and it has a validity period on the conditions. Rebate agreement is created before the rebate process starts from the sales order. It is accrual process and its credit gets accrued at the end of the process. SAP standard rebate agreement can be created based on Customer, Material, group rebate, and hierarchy types. Additional rebate agreement can be created with t-code, "VB(2 ". Rebate agreements have start date and end date. Rebate has a pricing accrual with pricing condition type.

> **Rebate is type of discount that is issued after invoice process.**

Change View "Rebate Agreement Types": Details

New Entries 📋 🖺 📝 🖳 🗒 🔩

Agreement | 0003 | Customer Rebate

Default values

Proposed valid-from	3	First day of year
Proposed valid-to	2	End of the current year
Payment Method		Default status

Control

Cond.type group	0003	Customer
Verification levels		Display all documents
☐ Different val.period		Rebate agreement and cond.record have same validity
ManAccrls Order type		☐ Manual accruals
Arrangement calendar		

Manual payment

Payment procedure	B	Payment allowed up to the value of the pro forma sett
Partial settlement	R3	☑ Reverse accruals
Settlement periods		

Settlement

| Final settlement | B1 | | Correction | B2 |
| Minimum status | B | Agreement released for settlement |

Text determination

| TextDetermProc. | |
| Text ID | |

Sales Order Configuration:

Order type controls the sales document header level. Order type configuration configured with T-code VOV8. The customization for contracts, scheduling agreement, sales order, and credit/debit memo also uses the same configuration. So this section can be used a configuration guide for all sales documents, including: Sales orders, Contract, scheduling agreements, Credit and debit memo, Inquiry, and quotation. It is best practice to copy from start order type and customize it so it doesn't require recreating who whole order type, but it is critical to understand the controls so they can be utilized as per requirements.

Header level Sales document type customization:

This section will be covering quantity contact type customization.

Contract type QC is standard contract type.

Document category:

Document category defines what kind of document it is. It is a very first control in sales document customization, so it categorized the document type based on this value. Document category for Contract type is "G".

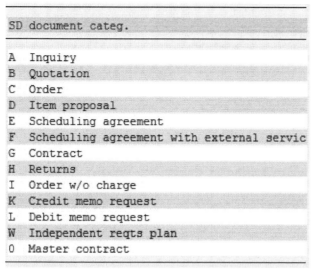

These values control the document type.

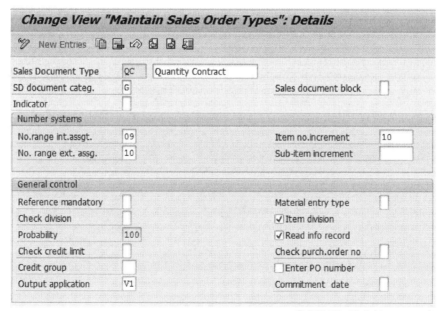

To Configure Sales Document the document category determines the sales document type.

Please follow the Figure "Sales Document Type".

```
SD document categ.

A  Inquiry
B  Quotation
C  Order
D  Item proposal
E  Scheduling agreement
F  Scheduling agreement with external servic
G  Contract
H  Returns
I  Order w/o charge
K  Credit memo request
L  Debit memo request
W  Independent reqts plan
O  Master contract
```

Sales Document Types for other document controlled with an element of the configuration.

Sales Document Block:

Sales document Block can be set by this field options. It can be set for credit notes in the process of approvals.

Indicator:

Indicator field can be set to control the document indication of the process. It classifies further controls of sales document type.

Indica	Short Descript.
	No classification
B	Delivery order
C	Scheduling agreement with delivery order
D	Invoice correction request
E	Delivery order correction
F	Repair processing: Leading serviceable material
G	Repair processing: Leading service product
H	Scheduling agreement with external service agent processing
I	Consignment issue by external service agent
K	Correct consignment issue by external service agent
R	Order for Billing Between Company Codes (RRICB)

Number Range:

The number range determines the sequence document number at the time of sales order creation. To able to identify between document types it is appropriate to assignee different number ranges, so it can help identification of document with different numbers.
Example service contract can start with 2000 and sales order can start with 3000 numbers so it is easy to identify just looking at document number and it also can help in reporting.

Two types of number ranges can be maintained in sales document customization: internal number range and external number range. The internal number range will auto populate and external number range is manually entered into a sales document. Item increment is for what next number should be inclement of the next number. Like if the order has increment of the first order is 20010 and second order is 20020.

General Control:

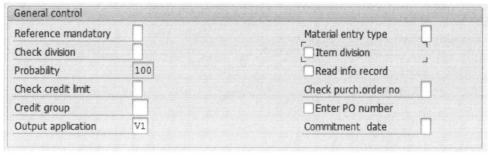

In "General Control" section 9 option for controls and three selection options.

Reference mandatory:

The reference mandatory control the reference document is required for preceding document and for the reference before going forward to create a sales order.

Check Division:

Check division error can be set to issue error at the time of creation of sales from warring, dialog, or no dialog display.

Probability:

This field is used for the planning of consumption based on probability set in sales order header type. It is used for inquiry and quotation to value the probability will be confirmed to be a sales order.

Check Credit Limit: Credit limit check controls for sales order level can be set here.

Credit Group: Documents can be assigned to different credit groups in this field.

Output Application: This selection field is used for outputs application identification.

Material entry control: This Selection field controls product catalog related controls if they want to activate product catalog in the sales order.

<u>**Check boxes:**</u>

> **Item division:** This check is required before saving or creating sales order.

> **Read Info Record:** check for the Customer Material Info record, so with this selection sales order will check CMIR.

> **Enter PO Number:** If this check is set, it will make Purchase order field required in the sales order document.

Check, Purchase Order Number:

This function checks if any purchase order already exists to avoid duplication of same purchase order in the system.

Commitment Date:

A number of factors are involved with different combination options. If the user selects the data, then system check for the stock and calculate delivery time and according to selected value system schedule commitment dates.

Transaction Flow:

Transaction flow				
Screen sequence grp.	LP	Outline agreement	Display Range	UALL
Incompl.proced.	12	Outline Agreement	FCode for overv.scr.	UER1
Transaction group	4	Contract	Quotation messages	
Doc. pric. procedure	Ö		Outline agrmt mess.	
Status profile			Message: Mast.contr.	A
Alt.sales doc. type1			ProdAttr.messages	
Alt.sales doc. type2			☑ Incomplet.messages	
Variant				

Transaction flow has controls on the sales document processing with required filed, Pricing, alternative sales order types, messages, transaction group, Open contract check, document completeness messages, and more.

Document Pricing Procedure:

It is used for pricing determination from sales document controls. Document pricing indicator helps pricing determination procedure to get determine in sales document.

Alternative Sales Order Type:

Two or more alternative sales order types can be configured. Users can specify alternative sales order types in these fields if an order is required to be saved with different sales order type. With this, sales order type can be changed after the sales order sales.

F-code default for overview screen:

This can be set to display sales order header tab screen as default screen to start order entry. If a user wants to start the order with "ordering party" tab, then the value of need to be set here to get the "Ordering tab" as a first screen?

Message: Master Contract:

This feature is used to enable if the system needs to check if a master contract exist.

Outline Agreement Message:

This feature is used to enable if the system needs to check if an open contract exist at the time of sales order creation and display a message.

Quotation Message:

This feature is used for display a message if the system needs to check if open quotation exist at the time of sales order creation.

Incomplete Procedure:

Incomplete procedure uses "incompletion log" configuration settings here for the sales document. Incompletion log setup is separate configuration, it can be set to make field in the sales document required and optional.

Screen Sequence Group:

Screen sequence group selection controls the display, which screen needs to be displayed and what sequence they will be displayed, can be identified with appropriate sales orders categories.

Transaction Group:

The transaction group identifies or separates a document from categories like: Contract, scheduling agreement, sales order, and item proposal.

Scheduling Agreement:

This section is for scheduling agreement. The sales document type has four customizations.

Scheduling Agreement		
Corr.delivery type	Delivery block	
Usage		
MRP for DlvSchType		

- Correction Delivery Type
- Usage
- MRP for Delivery schedule type
- Delivery Block

Correction delivery type specifies which delivery order type will be used to correct delivery for the scheduling agreement. Usage is used for material usage for order type at header level and it will be determined in all the line item. Material requirement planning is set active MRP requirements for delivery date confirmation with agreement dates. Delivery block uses to set delivery block initially at the time of the creation of the scheduling agreement.

Shipping:

Shipping		
Delivery type		Immediate delivery
Delivery block		
Shipping conditions		
ShipCostInfoProfile		

This customization controls deliveries and shipments. Shipping controls shipping relevant delivery types. If an order needs to be on the delivery block and shipping condition, set at header lever. These are the following controls are in shipping control tab.

- Delivery Type
- Delivery Block
- Shipping Conditions
- Shipping cost info profile
- Immediate delivery

Delivery Type:

This specifies what type of delivery can be created against sales order, additional configuration may be required for copy control setup.

Delivery Block:

Delivery block sets delivery block in the sales order. If delivery block has set them sales order will be created by delivery block, and delivery cannot be created until this block is removed.

Shipping Conditions:

Shipping Point can be assigned at sales order header level.

Shipping cost info profile:

This profile setup pricing determination in delivery from sales order.

Immediate Delivery:

If this option is selected, delivery will be created at the time of sales order creation. Example: The rush order requires immediate delivery, with this option selected delivery document will be created as soon as sales order is created.

Billing:

Billing has controlling elements similar to order type controlling elements. Additional sales order header controls order and delivery related billing options.

Billing			
Dlv-rel.billing type		CndType line items	
Order-rel.bill.type		Billing plan type	
Intercomp.bill.type		Paymt guarant. proc.	
Billing block		Paymt card plan type	
		Checking group	

Delivery related Billing Type:

This option makes a sales order for delivery related billing. Delivery type will be entered in this field.

Order Related Billing:

Order related billing controls if the billing can be done as soon as sales order is created.

Intercompany Billing type:

Intercompany billing type controls used for intercompany sales order processes.

Billing Block:

This function controls billing block in sales order at the time of sales order creation.

Condition Type Line Item:

The pricing condition used for the pricing in sales order and billing document.

Billing Plan Type / Payment Card Plan type:

Billing plan is what kind of billing plan will be used from this ales order. Billing plan could be milestone billing or periodic billing or customized billing plan can be used here as well.

Payment Guarantee Procedure:

Payment Guarantee is used from order type for payment guarantee determination from it.

Checking Group:

Checking group determines payment card type processing functionality.

Requested Delivery Date / Pricing Date / Purchase Order Date:

Requested delivery date/pricing date/purchase order date	
Lead time in days ☐	☐ Propose deliv.date
Date type ☐	☐ Propose PO date
Prop.f.pricing date ☐	
Prop.valid-from date ☐	

Here we configure parameters to set date in sales order which are relevant pricing related functions.

Lead Time in days:

Number of days are proposed in the sales order for the lead time. The number values used to define days needed to be calculated.

Date Type:

Date type is a selection option. Data types could be in days, weeks, months, posting period and year.

Purposed Pricing Data:

Price validity can be set on the following:

- Contract Data
- Valid from data
- Required delivery date

If no values maintain then price effective date will be from toadying, meaning sales order creation date.

Purpose validity of data:

If no values maintain then date effective date will be from toady, meaning the sales order creation date. Validity date is set for quotation data, that validity data will be effective for sales order processing.

Purpose delivery date / Purpose PO data:

For delivery dates, the proposal check box is selected. Then the system will populate today's date in the sales order. If the Purpose PO check box is selected, then the system will carry out todays date in the sales order.

The important configuration in this section is **pricing date.**

Contract:

Following contract section will be covered in detail with field level descriptions. Contract screenshot is the following.

Pricing procedure condition Header:

Pricing procedure purposed from "Pricing procedure condition header" field selection options.

Pricing procedure condition Item:

Pricing condition type for contract purposed from "Pricing procedure condition item" field selection options.

Contract Profile:

This profile selection is used for valid date of the contract, start and end date are part of profile setup.

Billing Request:

Billing request type selected, for example, credit memo.

Group Reference procedure:

Group reference procedure used in the master contract. This procedure required for identical field, copy field and configuration between contract types with master data setup.

Contract Data Allowed:

If selection is selected, then contract date can be manually entered in the sales order.

Follow-up Activity Type:

Customization sets up follow-up document procedure after this contract is created.

Subsequent Order Type:

The subsequent order type identifies what is the next document should be used for the contract.

Check Partner Authorization:

This will check for valid partner is used for the contract.

Update Low level Contract:

This check box controls if the high-level contract should change the low level contract. If it is selected in master contract, then it will carry out changes in all the contracts are under it.

Availability Check:

This setting is relevant for the APO availability check.

The sales order configuration will be the very similar to contracts order type configuration but with different variations according to order type. Order type has header level controls and any customization will affect the all the lines in sales document. For additional and secondary level control item category customization will effect for that line level based on item category group. Order type customization with t-code VOV8.

Some of Standard Order types are:

Order Type	Description
OR	Standard Order type
RE	Return order
CR	Credit Request
DR	Debit Request
FOD	Free of Delivery
RO	Rush Order

Sales Order Related T-Code:

T-code	Description
VA01	Create Sales Order
VA02	Change Sales Order
VA03	Display Sales Order
VA05	Sales Order Report
SD01	Sales order report with date range
V.02	Incomplete Sales Orders (Report)
V.15	Backorder report

Sales Order Screenshots:

The following screenshot of sales order is without customer master and material master information. Customer Master is used in Sold to field and Ship to field.

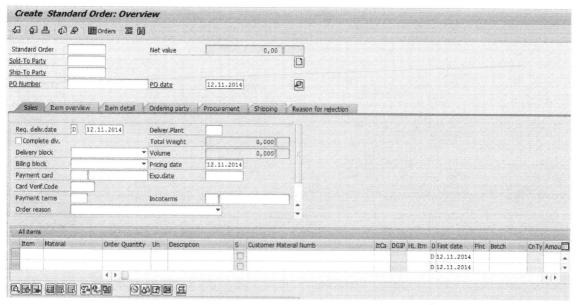

Sales Order Structure:

Sales Order has many controls from header, Item and Schedule Line and following figure represents the high level overview of the sales order.

- Sales order header information flow into sales order item information and schedule line.
- Header information applied to all the lines but at line level information can be changed.
- Schedule lines can be changed separately

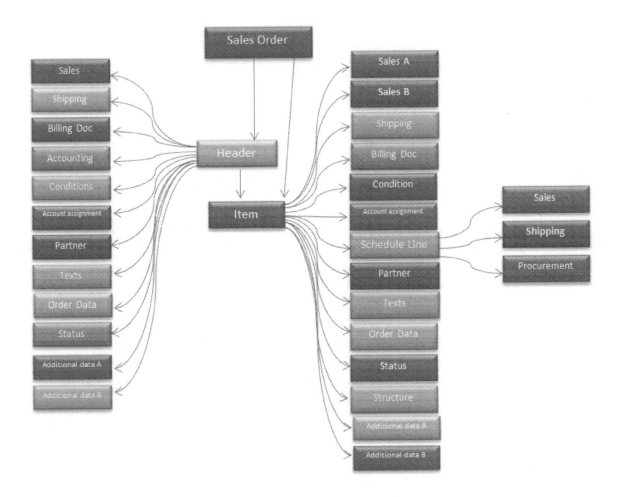

As the screenshot represents the how header information drives down to the item level, it goes and effects item and schedule lines, but additional functionality at item level item category and schedule line category can differ from the header. Item also receives direct input for material independent of the header.

Sales Order

Sales order header and Item information are available from t-code VA01 or VA03:

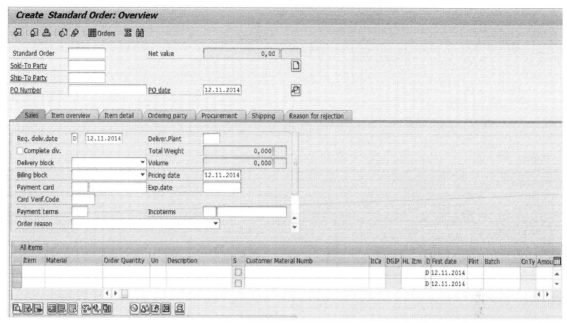

Sales Order Header with Tabs:

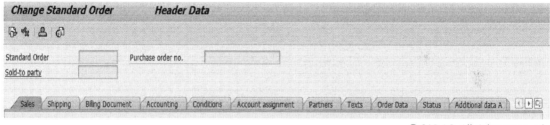

Sales Order can be viewed in detail via clicking this button

Sales Order with Item Tabs:

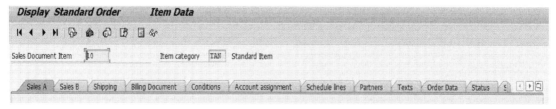

Item Category Customization:

Item Category controls the behavior of sales order line level. Line Item is like a mini sales order line level, and it is dictated by order type then item category. Item category customized with T-code VOV7.

IMG → Sales and Distribution → Sales → Sales Document → Sales documents Item → Define Item Category   T-code: VOV7

Change View "Maintain Item Categories": Details

New Entries

Item category	TAN	Standard Item

Business Data

Item Type		☑ Business Item
Completion Rule		☑ Sched.Line Allowed
Special Stock		☐ Item Relev.for Dlv
Billing Relevance	A	☐ Returns
Billing Plan Type		☑ Wght/Vol.Relevant
Billing Block		☐ Credit active
Pricing	X	☑ Determine Cost
Statistical value		
Revenue Recognition		
Delimit. Start Date		

General Control

☐ Autom.batch determ.   ☐ Rounding permitted   ☐ Order qty = 1

Transaction Flow

Incompletion Proced.	20	Standard Item	Screen Seq.Grp	N
PartnerDetermProced.	N	Standard Item		
TextDetermProcedure	01	Sales Item	Status Profile	
Item Cat.Stats.Group	1	Order, Debit Memo	☐ Create PO Automatic.	

Bill of Material/Configuration

Config. Strategy		
Mat. Variant Action		☐ Variant Matching
ATP material variant		
Structure scope		☐ Create Delivery Group
Application		☐ Manual Alternative
		☐ Param. effectivities

Value Contract

Value contract matl	
Contract Release Ctrl	

Service Management

Repair proced.	

Control of Resource-related Billing and Creation of Quotations

Billing form		DIP Prof.

- Item category controls billing type, (if item is for billing relevant or not)
- Item category customization used for line item controls.

- Pricing relevant
- Type of Item
- Incompletion rule
- Stock type
- Relevant for delivery
- Credit control
- Resource related billing controls
- Control for variant
- Bill of Material controls
- Item relevant for return
- Variant Configuration material

Item Type:

Item type is a first customization object in the item category configuration.

Item ty...	Short Descript.
	Standard Item
A	Value Item
B	Text item
C	Packing item (will be generated)
D	Material not relevant
E	Packaging Item (External)

If the value maintained as "B", then system considers it as text item. Packaging material Item type is C. With this customization transaction process changes and system behavior changes.

Completion Rule:

Item category can be found at the sales order level. It creates a sales order and the line there should be an item category field. Item category effect many process and control item and schedule line determination.

Item category types:

Description	Item Category
The standard	TAN
Free Item category	TANN
Consignment fills up	KBN
Consignment issue	KEN
Consignment returns	KRN
Consignment picks up	KAN
Inquiry item	AFN
Quotation item	AGN
Scheduling agreement	LPN
Service item	TAD
Debit Memo Request	L2N
Credit Memo Request	G2N
Value contract item	WKN

Each of Item categories has different controls. These item categories should be used as a template to copy to a new item category.

Item Category Group:

Item category group is grouping of material master for sales process. Item category group is assigned to the material master. Item category group is assigned to the basic view and the sales org view of the material master. Based on the item category group item category get determine.

E.g.
Standard Item Category Group: NORM
Services and non-stock material. DIEN
Third party ordering Item Category Group: BARNS
for service contracts we need Material with Item Category DIEN,

Item category Determination:

Item category determines in sales order automatically based on following:

IMG → Sales and Distribution → Sales → Sales Document → Sales documents Item → Assign Item Category

Item category determines by four things:

- Order Type
- Item category group
- Usage
- Higher level Item category

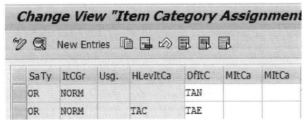

1. Order type comes from order creation.
2. Item category group come from material Master.

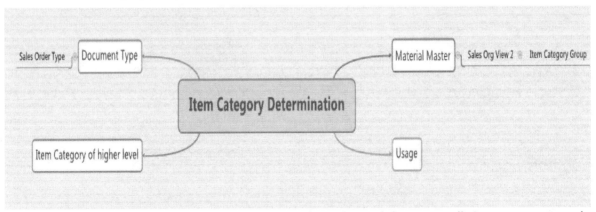

3. Default item category gets populated based on this and then manually item category can be allowed in additional fields, as in the above screenshot.

Usage: It can indicate usage of an item if it is a text item and return process.

Higher level Item category: Higher level item category used for Bill of material higher level item category or free good higher level item category.

Figure of item category determination:

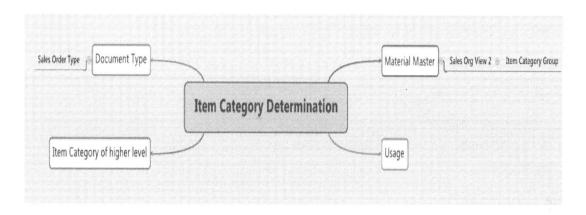

As it is shown in figure, item category is determined by four things in sales order, but two of them are required to determine the item category: order type and item category group. In the figure it shows the order type come from the sales order header and item category group come from material master.

Schedule Line:

Schedule line control, scheduling and MRP related element in the sales order.

IMG → Sales and Distribution → Sales → Sales Document → Sales documents Item → Assign Define schedule Line category

Schedule line controls the following element:

- Delivery Block
- Movement type
- Relevant for delivery
- Required / Assembly-relevant
- Availability-relevant
- Product allocation
- Third-party order Purchase Requisition

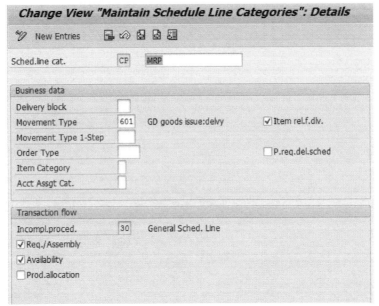

Delivery Block:

Delivery block can be set for the customized schedule line category. If this is set every line created with the schedule line will be created with delivery block.

Movement Type:

Movement type control system postings for each movement type, it effect debit and credit entries. Movement of good could be receiving, transfers, or goods are issued. Each movement type has postings set for it. In general, few movement types are used with schedule line.

601 Good Issues for Delivery
651 Delivery Return
631 Consignment Lending

Relevant for Delivery: That control if item relevancy for delivery so the schedule line is schedule line is scheduled.

Availability Relevant: It controls if the schedule line should pass requirements for availability check.

Product Allocation: This check box control if this schedule line needs to be relevant for product allocation.

152

Schedule Line Determination:

IMG → Sales and Distribution → Sales → Sales Document → Sales documents Item → Assign Schedule Line category

Schedule line is based on two things:

1. Item category
2. MRP type

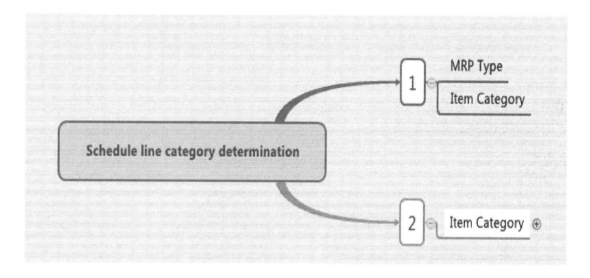

Item category and MRP determine item category determination. The system looks for item category and MRP type combination first. If not found, then system only can consider only item category. MRP type determines from material master MRP 1 view. MRP type determines what kind of planning is used for the material.

IMG → Sales and Distribution → Sales → Sales Document → Sales documents Item → Assign Schedule Line category

T-code: VOV5

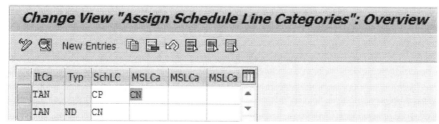

ItCa	Typ	SchLC	MSLCa	MSLCa	MSLCa
TAN		CP	CN		
TAN	ND	CN			

SAP Return Process RMA

- Introduction
- Business Process
- SAP process and Configuration
- Summary
- T-codes, Tip and issues on RMA

Introduction:

RMA stands for Return Merchandise Authorization. RMA process starts from when a customer wants to return an item. A return order is created if the sales order exists. The RMA process can be different based on business requirements and business process. Some business process requires a return authorization approval before customer return the merchandise.

Business Process:

The return authorization process is mainly based on how business operates. It depends how they would like to keep the process with their terms and conditions. When returning initiated, then customer contact customer service before return and they issue an RMA approval number to the customer and return label. When returning shipment is received back at the warehouse, it goes through the quality inspection and then it will be added back in inventory. After the return order good receipt, then credit will be issued to the customer.

SAP process:

In the SAP RMA process starts with creation of return sales order. After returning sales order, a return delivery will be created and a delivery document will be given to the customer as an RMA approval number. Few factors need to be considered such as what item categories are allowed and other copy control settings needed for the return process. RMA returns should have a sales order to reference to the return order also called RMA return material approval. For RMA some restrictions may apply according to the terms of customer and business. The return RMA is sales order RE created with t-code va01 and then return delivery is created and then credit memo issued to the customer.

Summary

The RMA process is a combination of business process and how it will translate into SAP. RMA is business process where return process is used from SAP.

T-codes

T-codes are used in RMA process are:

T-code for returns is VA01
Item Category Group: NORM
Item Category: REN

Consignment Process:

In consignment process, companies moves their inventory to customer locations, but ownership stay with the company and it will be counted in company stock. The stock is moved on the basis of condition, if product sold by customer then only it can be charged to the customer. If the customer did not sell then they will be picked back to the company's plant or warehouse.

The Consignment Fill-Up

Consignment stock transfer to customer location called consignment Fill-up. In consignment fill-up, sales order process material belongs to company transferred at customer location. Consignment fill-up order type follows up with delivery document. In the system the stock will be assigned by customer number so it can be tracked by customer stock levels.

Order type: CF

Item Category: KBN

Controls for Item Category: KBN

- Relevant for pricing: No
- Business Item: Yes
- Schedule Line allowed: Yes
- Weight/Volume Related: Yes
- Credit Check: No
- Cost: No
- Relevant for Billing: No

The schedule line states the item is relevant for deliveries. When the delivery is processed the item movement type is "631" at the time of goods issue, it posts the stock into a special consignment category.

The Consignment Issue:

The customer gets invoiced when a customer sells the materials. After customer informed about the product is being sold, then consignment issue order type is processed. With consignment issue processed liability transfer to the customer and in system invoice can be generated to the customer.

Order type: CI
Item Category: KEN

Controls for Item Category: KEN

- Relevant for pricing: Yes
- Business Item: Yes
- Schedule Line allowed: Yes
- Weight/Volume Related: Yes
- Credit Check: Yes
- Cost: Yes

Relevant for Billing: Delivery Related

The Consignment Returns:

In this Process consignment stock can be returned. Return processed based on when a customer wants to return the product at their location in the reference to consignment issue.

Order type: CONR

Item cat: KRN

Consignment Pickup

Consignment pickup is the process when the stock from customer sight taken back to the company, this process called consignment pickup. It followed inbound delivery and stock will reflect in the regular stock category.

Order type: CP

> **In Consignment process, stock is lend to the customer, if customer sells then we charge otherwise it will be returned.**

Plant Determination in Sales Order

The plant gets determination in sales order from following elements, plant gets to determine in sales order if these entries have value maintained in them. The system starts with following with priority.

1. Customer Material Info Record
2. Customer Master
3. Material Master

Plant Determination logic figure:

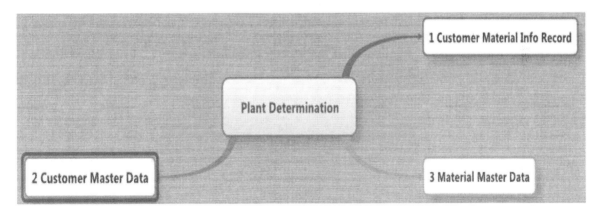

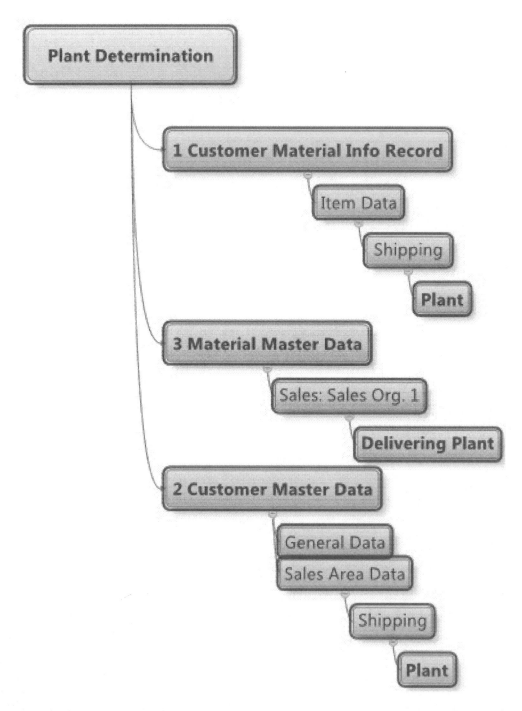

The system will check CMIR first if it contains Plant if not, then customer master if not then finally in the material master.

Customer Material Info Record

Customer material info record is maintained by t-code VD51. Customer Material Information record overwrite values from master data and present the most up to date information for sales document processing. The plant is maintained in the Customer Material Info Record at item level.

Customer Master

If customer maser sales view is the field value of delivery plant is maintained, then this will reflect in sales order.

Customer Master Screenshot (plant field)

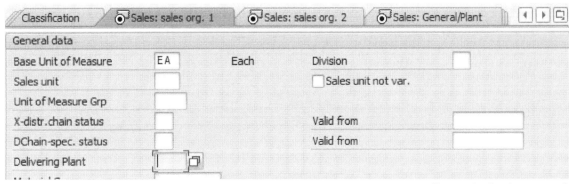

Material Master

If the field value of "delivering Plant" from the material Master view of "Sales: Sales Org 1" is available, then the plant value will reflect in sales order from Material Master.

Material master screenshot.

Dynamic Item Proposal:

Dynamic Item Proposal purposes item automatically based on order history, listing and exclusion material, item proposal, Customer material information record, and customer-specific master data.

The dynamic item proposal configuration is based on condition technique principle. The following are high level configuration elements:

- Define customer item proposal procedure
- Define document item proposal procedure
- Assign document procedure to sales document type.
- Table for Origin of product proposal
- Define a product proposal procedure
- Assign access sequence to the procedure
- Procedure determination for Background processing
- Procedure determination for online processing

IMG Customizing Path for Dynamic item proposal is
IMG → Sales and Distribution → Basic Functions → Dynamic Item Proposal

Customer Item Proposal Procedure:

Here we define Customer item product proposal procedure that gets assigned to the customer master and used in dynamic item proposal determination. The customer item proposal procedure is one of the elements that help automatic dynamic item proposal determination.

Customizing IMG path is
IMG → Sales and Distribution → Basic Functions → Dynamic Item Proposal → Define Customer Procedure for Product Proposal

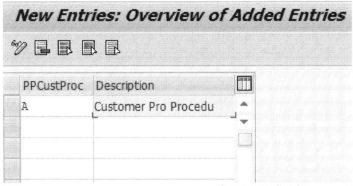

In above picture we can define product proposal customer procedure with alpha numeric with description.

Customer Product Proposal procedure Assignment:

The customer Product proposal procedure can be assigned in customer maser aster sales area data, under the sales tab. It can be assigned with XD01 or XD02.

Document Item Proposal Procedure:

The customizing path for Document Item Product Procedure is the following:

IMG → Sales and Distribution → Basic Functions → Dynamic Item Proposal → Define Document Procedure for Product Proposal

The Document Product Proposal Procedure can be created with a length of two characters, it could be alphabetic or numeric or a combination of both with the description.

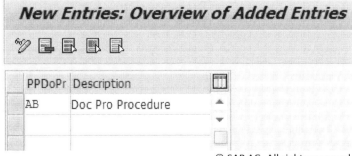

Assignment of Document Procedure of Sales Document Type:

Assignment of document procedure for sales document type can be assigned by following IMG path. IMG → Sales and Distribution → Basic Functions → Dynamic Item Proposal → Assign document procedure for Product Proposal to sales Document Type.

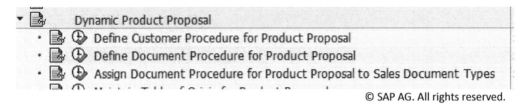

With this defined document procedure for product proposal will be assigned to the sales document type.

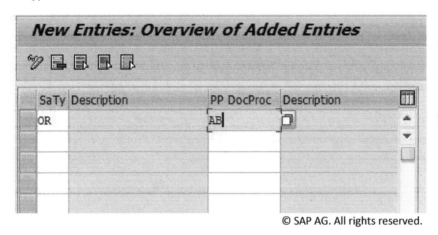

The above screenshot of the sales document type is getting assigned to document Product proposal procedure. With the assignment of Document product, procedure in the sales document it will be one of the elements to automatically determine dynamic item proposal.

Maintain Table of Origin for Product Proposal:

Customization for the table of origin of the product proposal is the following a path:
IMG → Sales and Distribution → Basic Functions → Dynamic Item Proposal → Maintain Table of Origin for Product Proposal

With the selection of the table, we are defining what source should be used for product to be proposed for, The following are predefine table entries can be used for the primary source for the origin of product proposal.

- Order History
- Listed Material

- Excluded Material
- Item Proposal
- Customer Material Info Record
- Customer-Specific data source

These sources used in sequence in which priority needed for the requirements in access sequence.

Define Product Proposal Procedure:

We start with the procedure because the access sequence is assigned to the product proposal procedure, so we need procedure first. To customized procedure following IMG guide path. IMG → Sales and Distribution → Basic Functions → Dynamic Item Proposal → Define Product Proposal Procedure

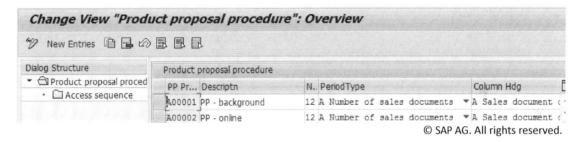

A00001 is the standard Product Proposal Procedure; it's a copy over for customization. The first field for control is "No. Of Per." **Number of Period** used for the history level if it requires looking back at 12 months or less, 12TH month is maximum period can be selected. **Period Type:** has a limit of the period need to be checked: number of documents, days, weeks, and month. **Column Header** also has the same values as Period Type. Assign Access Sequence to Procedure is the next step from the same customization. Assigning access sequence it needs functional module "SD_DPP_HISTORY"

> Dynamic item proposal will automatically display relevant item(s) or list of item(s) in sales order creation.

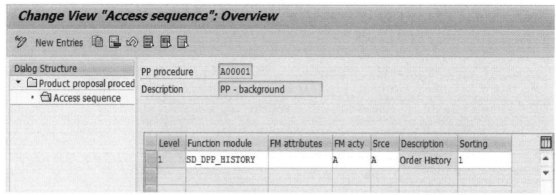

With access sequence it can be run with multiple sorting options. Sauces are from table sales order history, Listing, Exclusion as they are defined in table entries. Functional module used to look at the object history as per table entry. For Online the function module is SD_DPP_READ.

Procedure Determination for Background Processing:

Background processing determination IMG customization is the following:
IMG → Sales and Distribution → Basic Functions → Dynamic Item Proposal → Maintain Procedure Determination (In Background)

Background product proposal procedure determination is based on sales area with Product proposal customer procedure combination and it will determine background procedure based on it.

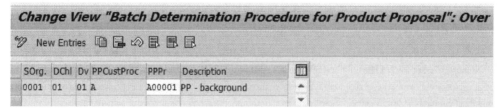

Above, the figure displays the sales area and Product proposal determination for back product proposal ground.

Procedure Determination for Online Processing:

Online processing determination IMG customization is the following:
IMG → Sales and Distribution → Basic Functions → Dynamic Item Proposal → Maintain Procedure Determination (online)

Online product proposal procedure determination is based on sales area with Product proposal customer procedure combination and it will determine background procedure based on it.

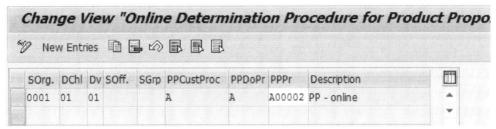

SOrg.	DChl	Dv	SOff.	SGrp	PPCustProc	PPDoPr	PPPr	Description	
0001	01	01		A		A	A00002	PP - online	

In above figure online product proposal determination is based on sales area sales, sales office, sales group, product proposal customer procedure and product proposal document procedure.

Item Proposal

Item proposal is used when a customer uses the same set of products in sales order repeatedly. Item proposal can have copy same quantity and can only copy materials in new sales order.
It can be used for the sales order fast entry to save time. Item proposal has validity start and end date. It proposal can be created with reference to sales order. Item proposal can be assigned to the customer master so the same item proposal will automatically propose for the sales order entry process.

T-code VA51   to create Item Proposal
T-code VA52   to change Item Proposal
T-code VA53 to Display Item Proposal
T-code VA55   Item proposal report

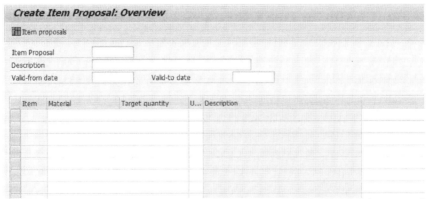

Item proposal Customization:

Item Proposal order type is "PV" to customize order type use t-code VOV8.

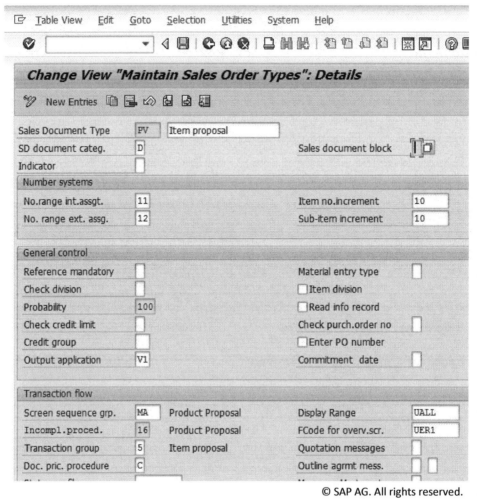

Following is customizable field are used, same as order type customization.

- Sales and distribution document category is "D" which is for item proposal.
- The number range is set accordingly to distinguish item proposal document type.
- Document pricing procedure is standard C.

Additional order type's related customization can be used for the item proposal order type.

Chapter 4 summary

- Learn about contracts and customization
- Learn about order type customization
- Contract Order type customization
- Learn about item category and schedule line determination
- Dynamic Item proposal Customization
- Item proposal Customization
- Plant determination
- Shipping point determination
- Learn about different return process
- Rebate agreement customization
- Delivery related report
- Shipping point determination

CHAPTER 5

DELIVERY & ROUTES

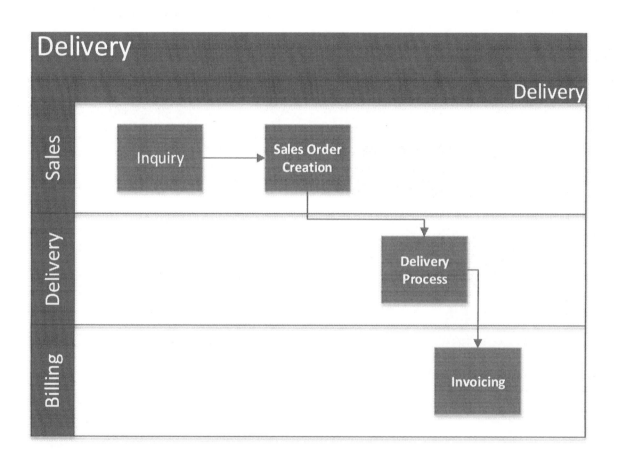

Shipment or shipping process called delivery in SAP

Delivery Customization

Delivery process is the following step of sales order or delivery can be created based on stock transfer order. Delivery integrate with sales and procurement modules. The scope of the topic is limited to sales related delivery. As we can see in the screenshot, delivery is part of logistic execution module.

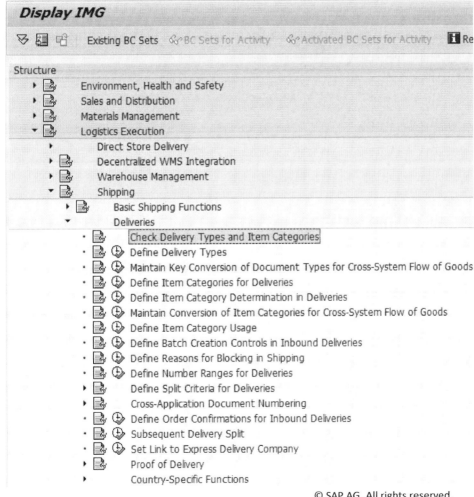

Delivery Type

Delivery type controls the delivery document behavior. Delivery type determines from sales order customization. In sales order it has delivery type defined in it. The standard delivery type is LF.

T-code: **OVLK**

Customization Path:

IMG → Logistics Execution → Shipping → Deliveries → Define Delivery Type

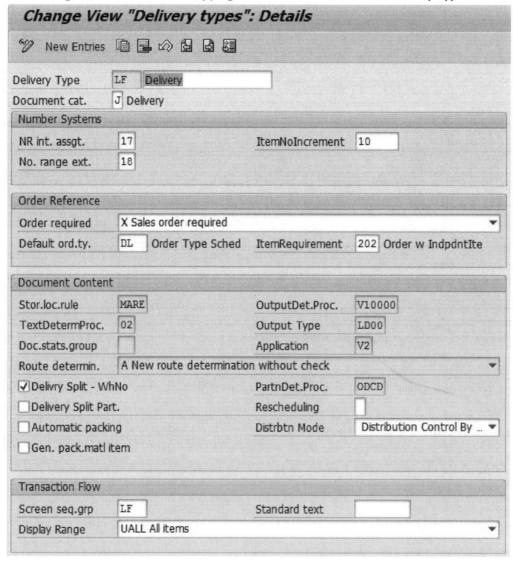

Document category:

Document category define type of delivery.

Order Reference:

This section of customization is customized if order required for reference or if returnable packaging required to be calculated.

Route Determination

Routes are setup for delivery, starting from the sales order. The mode of transport could be Air, Rail, Ground, Road, by Sea, and many others. The routes can be maintained for different type of product based on source, destination, priority, and weight group. The route time can be saved in SAP to be used for estimate routes in the sales order process for transportation.

Mode of Transport:

Mode of transport represents type of the transport. The type of transport could be Air, Sea, Train or more.

Customization Path from SPRO t-code is

IMG →Sales and Distribution → Basic Functions → Routes → Define Routes → Define Modes of Transport

T-code for customization: OVTB

Screenshot:

"S Ty" is a representational mode of transportation system number and followed by a description of it.

S Type Field represents a dangerous good mode of good category.

Define Shipment Type:

In this customization we are defining the shipment type with it can be included a mode of transportation and also transportation group.

Customization Path from SPRO t-code is:

IMG →Sales and Distribution → Basic Functions → Routes → Define Routes → Define Shipping Type,   T-code for customization: 0VTA

Screenshot:

Shipping types				
PT	Description	MdTr	Description	STPG
01	Truck	01	Street	
02	Mail	06	Postal Service	
03	Train	02	Train	

Define Transportation Connection Point:

Transportation Connection point brides when product transfer from one to shipment type another shipment type, the connection point could be Airport or border. The connection point also can maintain custom office description information in it.

Customization Path from SPRO t-code is:

IMG →Sales and Distribution → Basic Functions → Routes → Define Routes → Define Transportation Connection Point

T-code for customization: 0VTD

Screenshot:

Transportation connection point		
Points	Description	Cust.off.descr.
LOU	LOUISVILLE	
LVS	LAS VEGAS	

Define Routes and stages:

Customization Path from SPRO t-code is"

IMG →Sales and Distribution → Basic Functions → Routes → Define Routes → Define Transportation Connection Point

T-code for customization: 0VTC

Screenshot:

Route	[ ]

Identification

Description	[ ]
Route ID	[ ]

Processing

Service agent	[ ]		
ModeOfTr-Border	[ ]		
Shipping type	[ ]	Distance	[ ] [ ]
ShTypePrelLeg	[ ]		
ShTypeSublLeg	[ ]	☐ Rel.transport	

Scheduling

TransitTime	[ ]	Factory cal.	[ ]
Trav.dur.	[ ]		
TransLdTm.	[ ]		
TrLeadTimeHrs	[ ]		
AlwdTotWgt	[ ] [ ]		

Dangerous goods

☐ Take transit country table into acc.

Route: The route field defines the name of the route, it maintained by Z or Y field so the route stays with system upgrade.

Description: In this field, we describe about description about the route.

Route ID: This is and additional field where routes can be categorized for processing and description.

Processing: In processing controls the first field is **service agent**. The service agent field is used to define freight forwarder who facilitate the shipment. Service agent is defined as a vendor in system for shipment related services. The second field is used for processing controls is Mode of transport which is already being discussed in customization, the values are maintained in mode of transport can be used here. The third field is used for processing is **shipment type**, this field value already defined earlier in routing configuration and the values used for the route. The fourth and fifth field are primary and secondary shipment type legs of the route. The distance filed can maintain the distance of the route and unit of measure also can be maintained.

The last field in the processing section is "Rel. Transport". This control allows if delivery is relevant for shipment. If this is not selected, then the route will determine for delivery but these deliveries cannot be used in shipment.

Scheduling: This controls the duration and times of the route. The first field is used in scheduling controls is "Transit Time". The transit time is in days and it considers shipping point factory calendar for the calculation of transit time. The second field is used in scheduling control is travel duration, in this field, we maintain actual time in hours; this field value is not used in delivery scheduling calculation. The third field is transportation lead time based on the leading group and picking time, and value can be maintained with the consideration of shipping point time, transportation time in hours is fourth field. The fifth option is allowed total weight for shipment. The last value maintained is a factory calendar for the route.

Stages: Staging used for shipment additional steps like a border crossing and an additional step in configuration from the initial route definition. If in between shipments, an additional stage is required it can be configured in the router.

Define Stages For All Routes:

Customization Path from SPRO t-code is the following

IMG →Sales and Distribution → Basic Functions → Routes → Define Routes → Define Stages for All Routes

T-code for customization: 0VTE

Based on this configuration control it puts together many stages into routes based on the selection criteria.

Route Determination

Route determines by four elements in the sales order

- Country of departure / departure zone
- Country of Destination / Receiving Zone
- Shipping Conditions
- Transportation Group

Route determination for the delivery is same but also consider weight group for determining routes.

Customization Path from SPRO t-code is the following:
IMG →Sales and Distribution → Basic Functions → Routes → Route Determination

T-code for customization: 0VRF

Screenshot:

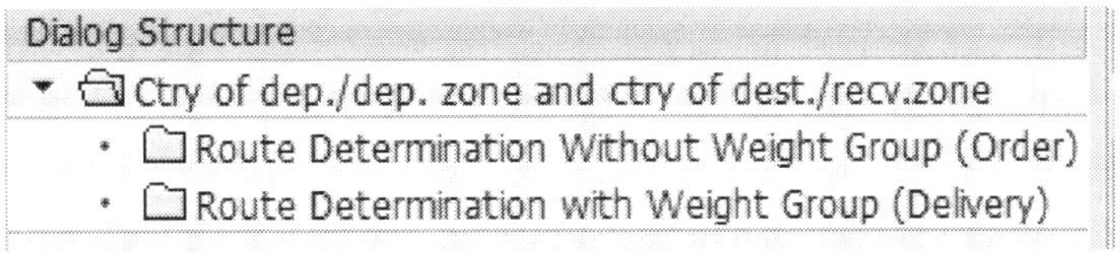

Field	Description
CDep	In the above screenshot the first field is "CDep", this represents the country of departure.
DepZ	"DepZ" field represents departure zone.
DstC	Destination Country
RecZ	This field is used for Receiving Zone

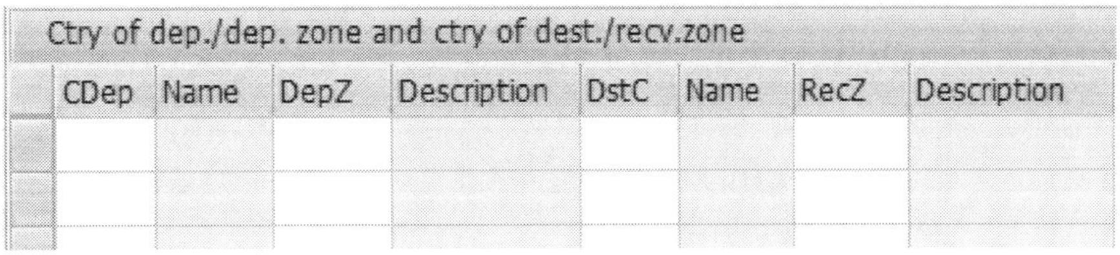

Tip to remember:

Departure Zone of Delivering Plant + Shipping Condition of the Sold to + Transportation Group + Transportation Zone of the Ship to

Define Transportation Zone

Transportation zone is defined and assigned to the customer master. This field value determines the route with a combination of other fields.

Customization Path from SPRO t-code is the following

IMG →Sales and Distribution → Basic Functions → Routes → Route Determination → Define Transportation Zone

T-code for customization: 0VR1

Screenshot:

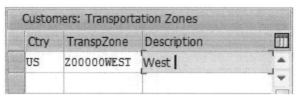

Define Transportation Zone for shipping point & Country.

Customization Path from SPRO t-code is the following:

IMG →Sales and Distribution → Basic Functions → Routes → Route Determination → Define Transportation Zone

T-code for customization: 0VR1

Screenshot:

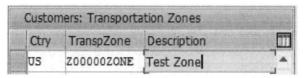

In the above screenshot we select the country and enter the Transportation Zone and the description of it.

Route determination figure:

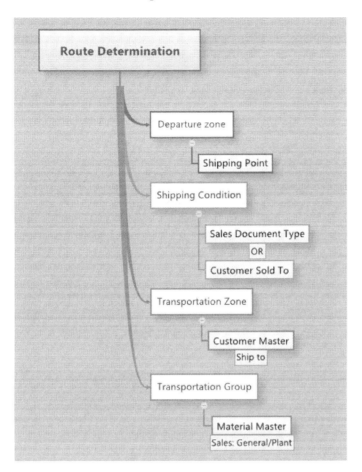

SAP SD Sales order Requirement Monitoring

Material master has MRP views that indicate functions of ATP and availability check. MRP controls if material is stock to order or make to order. If MRP is maintained to create requirements then it can tigers forecasting, production order, or create requirements to fill the order quantity. MRP can be activated by a schedule line category. The production order related to production planning module. Business production planning can pass the requirement to the respective module with system MRP planning. Production orders are subjected to MRP master data maintenance.

Delivery and Reports on Delivery

Delivery is part of general logistic execution module and shared across by logistics modules. Delivery has a different status based on the processing of delivery and what stage the delivery is at. Partial delivery means from sales order each line item or group of line items can be shipped separately. It can be a business requirement or customer requirement, as well in both cases sales order could have different ship to with separate lines to have different deliveries.

Partial delivery can be selected by sales order header option to be complete ship or partial ship. Delivery split happens due to different shipping point. Delivery due work list is used as report and monitor deliveries. Delivery monitor is one of the very useful tool to use to check delivery status too.

Shipping Delivery Monitoring T-code: VL06O

Delivery T-codes:

Description	Transaction Code
Create Outbound delivery	VL01N
Change Outbound delivery	VL02N
Display Outbound Delivery	VL03N
View Changes in delivery document	VL22
Delivery monitors	VL06O
Create In bound delivery	VL31N

Tip: The old t-codes do not contain "N" front of them, example: VL01

Delivery Related Tables

Description	Table
Delivery Header table	LIKP
Delivery Item Level table	LIPS
Delivery Note header	VBLK

Shipping Point Determination:

Shipping point determines where the product will ship from (Plant). Shipping Point determines at sales order line level. Shipping Point determination is an automatic process and it is based on three elements: Plant, Loading Group, and Shipping Conditions. The plant can be determined in sales order based on customer master or material master. The shipping condition comes on sales order line from customer master. Loading group element comes into a sales order line level from Material Master.

T-code: OVL2
IMG→ logistic Execution → Shipping →Basic Shipping Functions → Assign Shipping Points

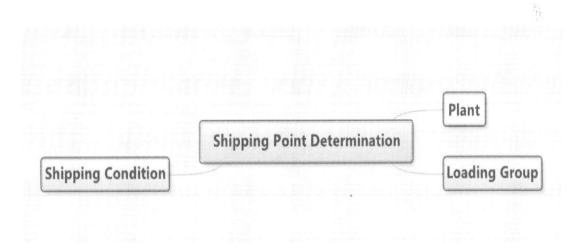

Shipping point determination *mind map*

Shipping point determination based on plant determination and that can be determine based on Customer, material, CMIR or ATP from APO.

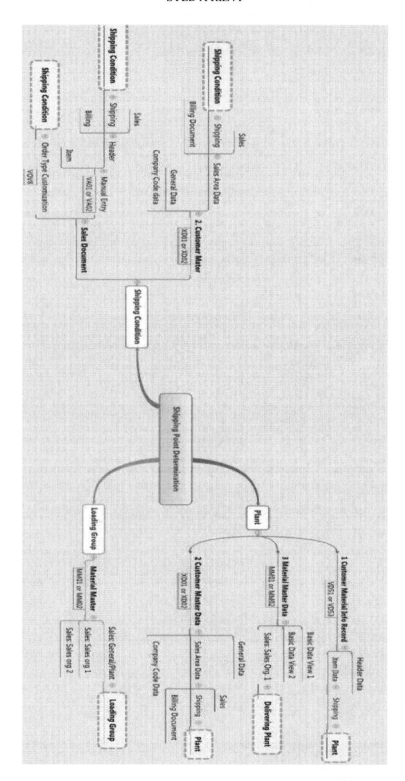

Configuration, customization:

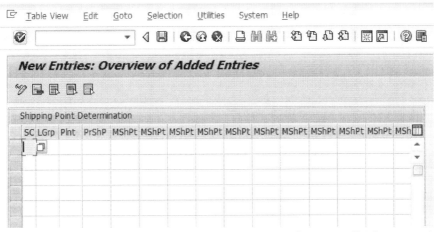

Shipping point get determine based on following:

Shipping Condition + Loading Group + Plant = Shipping point (additional shipping point can be added so they can be manually changed in the transaction)

Shipping Condition: is copy from customer master into sales orders.

Loading group: determines from Material Master.

The plant can determine from multiple locations, but mostly from material master.

Also the shipping point needed to be customized in the plant to process the transaction.

Chapter 5 summary

- Learn about contracts and customization
- Learn about order type customization
- Contract Order type customization
- Learn about item category and schedule line determination
- Dynamic Item proposal Customization
- Item proposal Customization
- Plant determination
- Shipping point determination
- Learn about different return process
- Rebate agreement customization
- Delivery related report
- Shipping point determination

Notes

CHAPTER 6

PRICING

Chapter 6 overview

- Pricing Fundamentals introduction

- Pricing Condition Technique

- Pricing Customization

- Customization of Pricing Table

- Customization of Access Sequence

- Customization of Condition Type (In detail)

- Customization of Pricing Procedure Deamination

- Introduction to Master Data Condition record

- Introduction to pricing routine

- Condition Record

- Listing / Exclusion Customization

-

SAP SD Pricing Fundamentals:

Introduction:

Price is used in sales, delivery, and billing processes. Price change often due to market cost of goods sold. Pricing is very critical part of any business. SAP pricing functions are based on condition technique customization. We need to understand the fundamentals of pricing and background how it works before can start customization. Pricing is a critical part of the sales order. Pricing effect account determination and revenue recognition. Pricing customization also used in billing, inquiry, quotation, and delivery. Pricing configuration also can be set with third party applications interfaces too.

Sales and Distribution's pricing is capable enough to handle simple and much complex scenarios. The standard pricing functionality is very flexible to handle many scenarios. Third party tools and applications available to integrate with, the pricing area to accommodate the complexity of pricing. In this chapter, we will focus on standard pricing configuration.

Condition Technique

Condition technique used in Sales and Distribution for various customizations. The condition technique provides conditional options to be given transactions for results based on the fields. In condition technique we create a table, then create an access sequence and assign table to access sequence, then assign an access sequence to condition, type, then put condition types in procedure and after that we create condition record. The pricing configuration is based on configuration technique. There is additional configuration required for advance pricing configuration and for account determination which is covered in billing chapter.

The high level objects of configuration are following:

1. Table
2. Access sequence
3. Condition type
4. Procedures
5. Condition Record   (condition type)

> **Pricing is used from presales to invoicing.**
> **SAP allow pricing in presales to invoicing.**

Condition Technique:

Table:

Any business condition can be converted into the field value. Condition technique is based on field or group of fields. The first step in condition technique processing is to create a table. A table could have one field in it or multiple fields. It is recommended to use existing tables if it is available if not then create a new table.

Access Sequence:

Access sequence is the place where multiple tables can be stored in it for access. To improve system performance, use minimum tables in access sequence and select exclusive option.

Condition Type:

The pricing Condition type is used to setup pricing. The pricing Condition type used for following type categories: Price, discount, freight, surcharge, and tax. The condition type has condition record with validity period. Many selection options are available to choose from, how the condition type can be used.

Pricing Procedure:

Pricing procedure controls the condition types in calculations and totals in it. It is 16 steps of configuration and can be controlled with combination of complexity.

Pricing Customization

Pricing configuration elements are followed:

- Pricing Table
- Access Sequence
- Condition Type
- Pricing Procedure
- Pricing Procedure determination

Pricing Table:

The SAP standard system already has around 600 entries of table that can be used. A table consists of single or multiple groups of fields in it. For customization tables can be created, after 600 because first 600 are reserved for standard table entries.

T-code for customization V/03

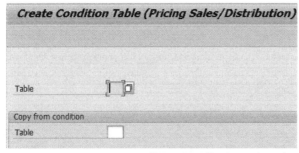

The table number is required to create a new table, and new table can be copied from existing tale to begin with for the changes.

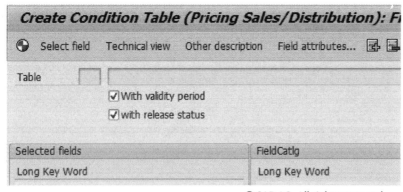

In the above screenshot, red and white buttons can be used to generate tables.

Access Sequence:

Access sequence is considered search criteria and the access sequence contain tables. Access sequence has a condition in tables so the field can be searched with the table combination of fields. Access table entry can be set for exclusive for system performance to stop searching based on found combined condition. Requirements is also used in access sequence for free goods, payer, currency, domestics, exports, and many other business processes.

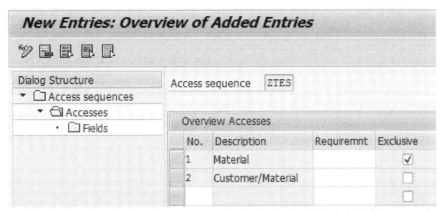

Tip: To navigate, select access sequence and click on the folder to go into access, and also table entries require additional enters to bypass soft error for table into a table.

Condition Type:

Condition type represents price, discount, taxes, freight, and surcharge on sales order. Each line can has multiple pricing conditions assigned to it. Pricing conditions can be further divided into different types of condition types: group condition, header pricing condition, and item pricing condition. The following are some of the pricing condition types:

- Price
- Discount
- Taxes
- Surcharge
- Freight

Business Use:

Each line can have the multiple price condition. For example, using one pricing condition could be for MSRP and one could be for current price based on a percentage of MSRP. There are also a couple of discount condition types, one discount and second one off of first discount condition. Condition types can fix price or percentage base. Pricing condition can be used for header level or item level. The difference between header and item condition is that header condition applied to the whole document and item condition applied to the each line level. Header condition divides the header amount into all the lines.

Condition Supplement:

Condition supplement is used for group conditions to be determined together. Based on one condition type, relevant supplement conditions will determine together. The condition types should have same pricing procedures in condition type setup. The condition supplement created with Transaction Code VK11

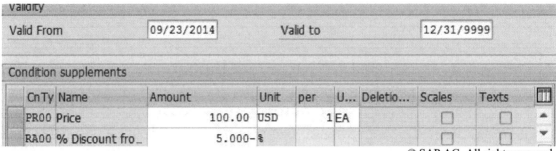

In the above screenshot, the condition record can be created for multiple condition type at once. From the configuration standpoint, the key element for condition supplement is to have condition pull together is the pricing procedure assign to the condition type. Following is the screenshot of the Master data section of condition type customization; the default value is "PR0000".

Customization:

Customization can be used for
IMG → Sales and Distribution → Basic Functions → Pricing → Pricing Control → Define Condition Type
The standard price condition is PR00

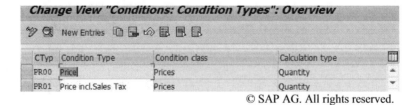

Condition Type: PR00

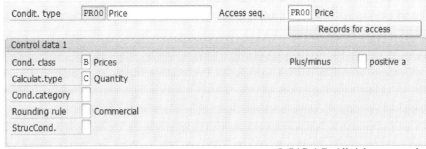

Access sequence:

Access sequence, as we studied earlier, it is used in pricing condition type. The access sequence determines the table.

Condition Class:

Conditional class classifies condition type, for example surcharge, discount, tax, etc.

Plus/minus: This identifies that if condition values are positive or negative or both.

Condition Category:

Condition category clarifies condition type category. For example Tax condition category can be selected.

Rounding rule:

Rounding rule round of value to closest decimal point (third place) or round down or keep it commercial. If value selected round down system will not consider any value from decimal point and keep it as is. For round up any value higher than five from third decimal point will increase one value to the two decimal point value.

Structure Condition:

This configuration used for variant condition if condition type needs to be duplicated or accumulated.

Additional Condition Type Controls:

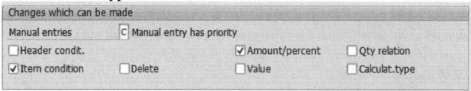

Group Condition:

Group condition is used when materials belong to the same group or price is set on the item in the group. It is for the item level of group material for pricing.

Example: if material A and B are belong to the same group and price is set to scale of ten for the group of materials together, then both material quantities can be mixed and matched and sale price will be effective for the group of the materials.

Group Condition Routine:

Routine is used for group condition or can be selected for non-group condition type.

Round Different Comparison:

This customization activates rounding calculation. It will start with header level, then condition level, and add to the condition with high value condition type.

Additional Condition Type Controls:

Changes which can be made			
Manual entries	C Manual entry has priority		
☐ Header condit.		☑ Amount/percent	☐ Qty relation
☑ Item condition	☐ Delete	☐ Value	☐ Calculat.type

Manual Entries: This customization allows manual entry for the condition type. This customization allows a number of options for manual entries. "C" manual entry has priority if this option, customized manual entry is allowed for the condition type and based on this if manual price is entered then it will overwrite the condition record. If option is left empty, then it has no limitation means it can be overwritten without limitation. If "B" is selected, then condition record has priority over the manual. "D" option doesn't allow any manual entry for the condition type. The value is distributed based on net value.

Header Condition: If this customization is selected it will make it header condition. Header condition manually entered at header level. Header condition distributes its values into all items.

Amount / Percentage: This customization defines amount or percentage to be changed during processing. If this is not selected the amount and percentage cannot be changed.

Quantitative relation: It customization allows units of measure to be change in pricing.

Item Condition: Item condition identifies if condition type is at item level. It will only be unique to the item it has been entered for.

Delete: This customization will allow the item's condition to be deleted from the document.

Value: This customization allows value can be changed during processing.

Calculation Type: This customization controls the calculation type, it changes during the processing.

Additional Pricing Controls with Limits:

Valid from:

Valid from date is for the condition type to be valid from.

Valid to:

Valid to date is the validity of condition type.

Scale Basis:

The scale customization can be set for the condition type if it is required to be based on quantity or in weight or in volume.

Check Value:

This customization is used for the descending or ascending price scales.

Condition Limit:

Condition limit customization limits the value. The value does not surpass percentage or quantity or weight. Example for discount condition type can be limited to the limit so over or under discount is not given when user is using manual ever written on condition type.

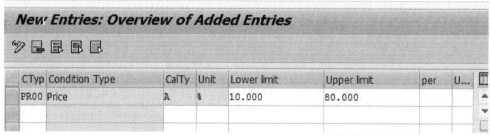

CTyp	Condition Type	CalTy	Unit	Lower limit	Upper limit	per	U...	
PR00	Price	A	%	10.000	80.000			

In the above screenshot the pricing limit can be set with calculation type unit percentage or quantity or weight, lover and upper limit, as per unit and unit of measure.

Pricing Procedure:

Pricing procedure customization based on the condition type calculation and functions. Pricing procedure has 16 steps of control for each line. It is always recommended to copy existing SAP pricing procedure with "Z" or "Y" so it will stay with system upgrade.

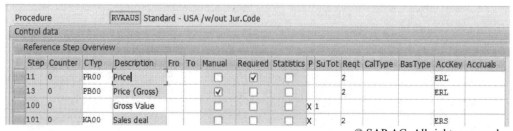

Procedure RVAAUS Standard - USA /w/out Jur.Code

Control data

Reference Step Overview

Step	Counter	CTyp	Description	Fro	To	Manual	Required	Statistics	P	SuTot	Reqt	CalType	BasType	AccKey	Accruals
11	0	PR00	Price			☐	☑	☐		2				ERL	
13	0	PB00	Price (Gross)			☑	☐	☐		2				ERL	
100	0		Gross Value			☐	☐	☐	X	1					
101	0	KA00	Sales deal			☐	☐	☐	X	2				ERS	

16 Pricing Procedure field for customization:

1. Step
2. Counter
3. Condition Type
4. Description
5. From
6. To
7. Manual
8. Required
9. Statistics
10. Print
11. Subtotal
12. Requirement
13. Calculation Type
14. Base Type
15. Account Key
16. Accruals

Step:

Step is the sequence system start processing, pricing procedure. The first step starts with 10 and the second one 20 the reason for the steps to be numbered this way user can add nine steps before them and nine steps after 10 if customization is required in between condition type steps. It is always recommended to use steps in gaps so if required additional steps can be added.

Counter:

The center is one of additional places where steps can be repeated and with different counter and the same step with combination can be each new step.

Condition Type:

Condition type where we use condition type. This field is not required field and it can be left empty for other use in pricing procedure.

Description:

Description comes from condition type description. When condition type is not used, then the description field becomes free form to use and it is used for totals in group of condition types to be calculated and display in document processing at the header and item condition tabs.

"From" and "To":

"From" and "To" field are used to calculate in a selected range of steps to be calculated in that step.

Manual:

Manual option on pricing condition type to allow manual entry for the condition type. Similarly for the condition type, this is another control to allow manual over write for the condition type. If this is option is marked then the condition type allowed for manually overwrites.

Required:

Based on this option condition type become required for the document processing and if condition record is not found system will issue an error for the required condition type.

Statistics:

Statistics selection marks, a condition type for statistical use for the pricing in document processing. Some condition types are used only for statistical mean not effecting pricing of the document.

Print:

Print customization controls if a line needs to be printed in outputs.

Subtotal:

The subtotal field is used to subtotal condition types.

Requirement:

The requirement is a calculation program that provided by SAP form many formulas. New requirement can be added as per requirements. In-depth; detailed summary of the subject is out of the scope of the book.

Calculation Type:

It is similar to the requirement field. Calculation type also used in condition type customization, but it is not same as the pricing procedure calculation type. Calculation type also has many system predefine selections, but a new one can be introduced into a system with enhancements. Examples of Calculation type are: net value, cash minus tax, and initial price. The calculation type from condition type customization is similar to the customization but the pricing procedure has many additional calculation type options available.

Base Type:

The base type is similar to the calculation type and requirement field, it has many options to select from and additional option can be enhanced into the system if needed.

Account Key:

Account key is used for account determination for the condition type. This customization is used for financial revenue recognition as per condition type.

Accruals:

Accrual field customization used for tracking accruals against the condition type. In this field account key for the accruals can be customized.

Pricing Procedure Determination:

Path for customization is
IMG → Sales and Distribution → Basic Functions → Pricing Controls → Define and Assign Pricing Procedure

After the above selection it will give a selection for the each of the component to select from for customization.

Short Definition:

Pricing procedure determines the formula = sales area + Customer Pricing Procedure indicator + Document Type Pricing Procedure.

Figure how pricing procedure gets to determine:

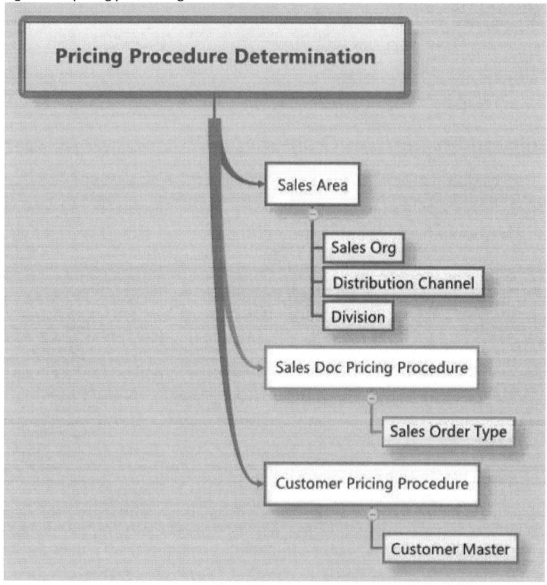

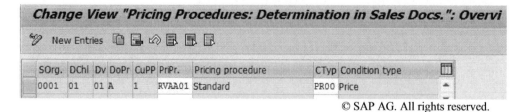

The determination components:

Sales area is = Sales organization + Distribution channel + Division + Division

Document Procedure Indicator:

IMG → Sales and Distribution → Basic Functions → Pricing Controls → Define and Assign Pricing Procedure → Define document pricing Procedure

Procedure document is a single alphanumeric character is assigned to the document type.

Step1: Create the document procedure or use standard pre define ("A" is standard)

Step2: Use T-code VOV8 for order type customization and add the document procedure to the document type.

Customers Procedure Indicator:

IMG → Sales and Distribution → Basic Functions → Pricing Controls → Define and Assign Pricing Procedure → Define customer pricing Procedure

The customer pricing procedure is a single alphanumeric character assigned to the customer master.

Step 1: Create the Customer pricing procedure or use standard pre define ("1" is standard).

Step 2: Use T-code XD02 and in sales are data and in sales Tab add pricing procedure indicator in it.

Pricing with System Performance consideration:

Pricing affects system performance when many tables are used in access sequence and system keep searching. The access sequence can stop searching with **exclusion** option and check box selection.

Condition Type limit can affect the system performance as well too. It can be avoided if the process is monitored and only selected condition types are used for this function. Access sequence optimization also one of the functions is provided by system to improve the search result and system performance.

Condition Record:

Condition record is based on the field used in condition table and based on it, we create master data of condition record with t-code of VK11 or VK31. The condition record could have a validity period. Condition record considered master data.

T-code for condition record	**VK11**
T-code to change condition record	**VK12**
T-code to display condition record	**VK13**

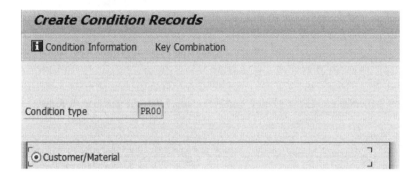

Condition Record:

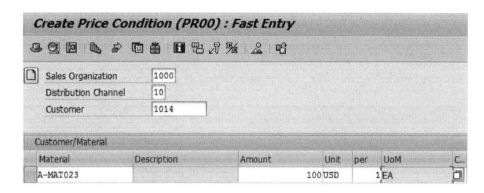

In the above screenshot condition record is created.

Condition record is pricing record saved using condition type. Base on the pricing setup and configuration, the condition record, master data can be created. Condition record has many controls for the condition type. Condition record can be created with T-code VK11.

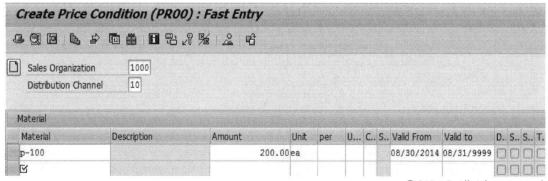

Condition record based on sales org and distribution channel, and based on access sequence the condition will be based on it. It has price for unit and valid from and valid to date. If condition record is deleted the "D" check box will be selected. The first "S" represent condition supplement. The second "S" represent scale Pricing. The forth check box "T" represent Text. These options will come from if the additional option are allowed in customization and added in condition record creation.

Tables for Condition record are following:

KONV for Document
KONP for Item Condition

Field Catalog

When new field needed to be added into the field catalog, then it needed to be added into the structure of the following table. After table entry into the field catalog and then the new field is available for table creation in the pricing table.

Advance level tables for customization structures:

1. KOMG
2. KOMK
3. KOMP

SAP Pricing Routines:

What is SAP pricing Routine?

Introduction:
Routines are small enchantment programs. Routines are written for pricing procedures, condition type and many more objects in customization. Pricing Procedure contains routine customization. Pricing procedure has SAP standard formula and calculation type. In sixteen steps in pricing procedure, few fields has formulas and calculation type can be categories as routines. New routines can be written and used for the pricing and other customizations.

Routines:

Enhanced routines are written in ABAP Advance business application programing language. Pricing routine can be viewed and written by using T-code VOFM. The routine could be related to calculation type, requirement and base type field of pricing procedure.

Use of Routine

Pricing routines can be used in the calculation type field in the pricing procedure set or subtotal or requirement type and condition formula for basis. We can use existing available routines, but if the requirements cannot meet with standard routines, then we create the new enhancement of routine.

Pricing in Order to cash:

Sales and Presales:

Pricing can be customized and used in presales process. Some business used inquiry document pricing copy to quotations pricing and that copy over to the sales order. So pricing setup can be customized before sales order and the configuration is similar to sales order customization. Price can be changed from inquiry to quotation and there would be price change. The sales pricing customization is flexible.

Delivery:

Delivery has freight and handing related pricing condition setup and this pricing condition copy over to invoice. Pricing in delivery is optional.

Invoice:

Pricing in invoice is copied over from sales order, but Pricing can be recalculated in invoice.

Pricing is very flexible it can be customized in Most of order to cash cycle process. Pricing copy over from document to document and each document can update the pricing based on business requirement.

Summary for Chapter 6

We cover in this chapter pricing, customization with standard setup with detail to the field level definitions.

- Pricing table customization
- Access Sequence customization
- Condition Type customization
- Pricing Procedure Customization
- Condition record
- Pricing determination

Notes

CHAPTER 7

BILLING & CREDIT MANAGEMENT

Chapter 7 Topics

- Introduction to Billing
- Customization in Billing Document
- Copy control
- Billing Reports
- Resource Related Billing
- Credit and Debits
- Charge back
- Pricing in Billing
- Billing Plan
- Credit Management
- Revenue recognition

Introduction to Billing:

Billing is one of the last steps in order to cash cycle, followed by order or delivery. Billing can be based on orders when we look into service industry billing is based on order or contract. From a customization standpoint, billing could be based on delivery. Billing is an integration point between FICO and SD Sales and Distribution.

Billing Customization:

Billing type customized from the billing order type. Additional customization can be done with item category customization. Sales order type has billing type define into it and based on the order type billing type determines in order to cash cycle. Pricing can also be reprocessed in billing.

T-code for billing Customization is **VOFA**
SPRO
IMG → Sales and Distribution → Billing → Billing Document → Billing Document Types

The standard billing document type is **"F2"**
Customization of billing document is the same framework for all the billing type but with different values. If all the fields are understood all other billing types can be understood easily. The customization of F2 document is the following.

Billing Type	F2	Invoice		Created by	SAP

Number systems

No.range int.assgt.	19		Item no.increment	

General control

SD document categ.	M	Invoice	☐ Posting Block
Transaction group	7	Billing documents	☑ Statistics
Billing category			
Document Type			
Negative posting		No negative posting	
Branch/Head office		Customer=Payer/Branch=sold-to party	
Credit memo w/ValDat	☐	No	
Invoice list type	LR	Invoice List	
Rebate settlement			☐ Rel.for rebate
Standard text			

General Controls

Number Range: The number range field controls which number will be used for the billing document.

IMG → Sales and Distribution → Billing → Billing Document → Define number range for billing document.
T-code for number range is VN01

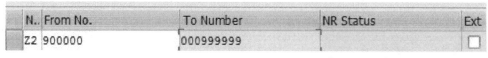

N..	From No.	To Number	NR Status	Ext
Z2	900000	000999999		☐

Ext: In the number range, Ext represents an external number range define that billing can be created with manually entered number. If Ext is not selected, then the system picks the next available billing number. Billing document number increments can be defined so the next number can be automatically created according to the controls.

SD Document Category:

The Sales and Distribution document category is the document type that representation type of document. "M" represents invoice which is a standard document type of invoice.

Posting Block:

Posting block can be set so when the billing document is created it will have a billing block in it. This control blocks any posting for the billing document.

Transaction Group:

Transaction group is also similar to the Document category field. It categorizes the document type by its group and processing functions with the group.

Statistics:

This checkbox controls if the billing document required for reporting and statistical use.

Negative Posting:

This field controls if negative posting is allowed. If negative posting is allowed or if not allowed, it can be controlled from this field.

Invoice list:

An invoice can be processed groups or batches. The invoice list, type in F2 billing is "LR". The invoice list allows group processing of invoices.

Rebate Settlement and Related for Rebate:

These two fields relevant for the rebate process. What type of rebate settlement is used for the billing document type, and if the billing document is relevant for the rebate related accruals.

Controls for Cancelation of billing document:

Cancellation		
Cancell.billing type	S1	Cancellation of Inv
Copying requirements		
Reference number		
Assignment Number		

If "F2" billing type needs to be cancelled based on the billing type system will check in the billing document type controls and use the cancel billing type. Relevant controls are in the screenshot that the standard cancel billing type for "F2" is "S1".

Controls for Account Assignment / Pricing

The first field of these controls is an Account determination for the billing type. The field value is a standard account determination procedure used in the screenshot is "KOFI00" and document procedure is used for pricing is "A". Document procedure is used if pricing required to be recalculated in billing.

Account assignment/pricing		
AcctDetermProc.	KOFI00	Account Determination
Doc. pric. procedure	A	Standard
Acc. det. rec. acc.		
Acc. det. cash. set.		
Acc. det. pay. cards		

Output / Partner and Texts Controls:

The first filed for customizations is "output determination procedure". It is used for output customization from billing type. The standard output condition type "RD00" is used in "Output type" field.

Output/partners/texts				
Output determ.proc.	V10000	Billing Output	Application	V3
Item output proc.				
Output Type	RD00	Invoice		
Header partners	FK	Billing Document		
Item partners	FP	Billing Item		
TextDetermProcedure	03	Billing Header		
Text determ.proc.itm	03	Billing Item		
☐ Delivery text				

For partner and text determination these are the standard fields are used for partner determination. "Delivery text field" copy text from a delivery document to the billing document text.

Invoice List

Invoice List is the process where billing documents can be processed together in a list, group, or batches. Invoice list was also used in billing document control and further additional customization can be used.

Assign Invoice list to the Billing Type:

IMG → Sales and Distribution → Billing → Billing Document → Invoice List → Assign Invoice List to Billing Type.

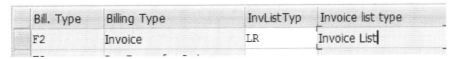

Bill. Type	Billing Type	InvListTyp	Invoice list type
F2	Invoice	LR	Invoice List

In this customization, invoice list is assigned to the invoice list type, based on this customization it will determine invoice list by billing type.

Copy Control for Billing Document:

Copy control copies appropriate values to proceeding document. The customization menu path can be followed by following Manu path from T-code SPRO:

IMG → Sales and Distribution → Billing → Billing Document → Maintain Copy Controls for billing Document

T-code: **VTFA**

Copy control is based on header level and item levels on the header level. It is based on the invoice type to sales order type level on item level it is based on item category level.

Target		Source	
Target Bill. Type	F2	Ref. SalesDoc Type	OR
	Invoice		Standard Order
Item Cat. Proposal		Item Category	TAD
			Service

Copy				
Copying requirements	002	Item/order-related	Billing quantity	A
Data VBRK/VBRP	001	Inv.split (sample)	Pos./neg. quantity	+
			Pricing type	G
			PricingExchRate type	
			Price source	

The source to target controls at header level and also and on the item category level.

Copy:

Copy controls field description is the following.

Copying Requirements:

The first field in customization is "Copying Requirements". The requirement is predefine program to choose from. The standard "copying requirements" value is "002" which represents that it is order related so billing is based on order.

Data BBRK / VBRP:

The data also similar filed as "Copy requirements" but the requirement is made for billing table "VBRP" billing item data and Billing header data table "VBRK" the standard requirement is used on "001" with controls for invoice split.

Billing Quantity:

Billing quantity controls which quantity should be copied into the billing document.

Positive and Negative quantity:

This customization allows positive or negative quantity to be copied over to the billing document.

Price type:

This customization determines if price need to be recalculated in billing or copy price element from the sales order.

Pricing Exchange rate Type:

This field controls what pricing exchange rate date is valid for billing. Pricing exchange rate could be based on order date.

Price Source:

Price source filed indicate where is price copied from the source of the price. Price source is based on order if left empty and also can be based on purchase order, delivery or external.

Billing Plans

Two different types of billing plans available in SAP

- Milestone Billing
- Periodic Billing

Milestone Billing:

Milestone billing is used where billing is issued for services in increments of services or billing issued based on milestone completion of services. For example, when building a house, the payment can be set for completion of each room or percentage and billing will be issued by milestone by milestone.

IMG → Sales and Distribution → Billing → Billing Plan → Define Billing Plan Type

T-code: **OVBI**

Billing plan type is 01 for the milestone billing.

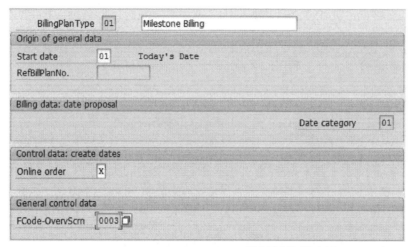

Start date: Select start from calculating date, using value "01" to represent todays date. When this plan is used in the document, it will consider the document date for the milestone billing needs to be start from.

Date category: This defines the processing date, also considering what type of date. 01 represents milestone relevant date, 03 represents down payment relevant date.

Online Order:

If "X" is marked, the system will purpose the dates, but when it is not marked the dates can be manually entered.

Periodic Billing:

Periodic billing is billing of service or product which is divided into periods of time. Periodic billing is like a rent payment on a house or product which is charged periodically.

IMG → Sales and Distribution → Billing → Billing Plan → Define Billing Plan Type

T-code: OVBI

BillingPlanType	02	Periodic

Origin of general data

Start date	12	Contract Start Date + 1 Week
End date	09	Contract End Date
Horizon	52	Horizon 1 Year
Dates from		
Dates until		

Billing data: date proposal

Next Bill. Date	50	Monthly on First of Month	Def. Date Cat.	01
Dev. Bill. Date				
Days in year		Days in month	Calendar ID	

Control data: create dates / invoice correction

Online order	X	In advance	☐	Aut.corr. dates	☐

Periodic billing has start and end dates that can be customized in the billing plan. The start date is based on: yearly, contract period, Billing date, contract validity + contract validity period, etc. The contract end date could be based on similar factors as contract start date. Horizon define is not the contract end date but it defined the length of the billing plan.

Dates "from" and "dates until" are the rule base dates determination. Next billing date controls when the next is billing date should be determined for the billing plan. The "Dev Billing Date" represents deviating billing date so the original billing date can be changed. For accounting the days in the year and days in a month can be set in these fields. Online order date allows automatic of manual entry. In Advance field allow billing in advance. The auto correction date field automatically corrects the invoice for the processing.

Credit Management:

On customer creation credit master issues a credit limit for sales process. The customer is allowed to do this with a credit limit. Credit limit automatically blocks transactions when the credit limit is reached. Credit functionality can be used to block sales order, delivery, and billing documents. Customer credit is calculated against the customer open document and credit exposure.

Credit master data controls the credit related transactions.

Credit Master:

Credit master is created with the combination of customer and credit control area. Credit is based on credit limit and credit risk assigned to the customer. Credit is calculated based on horizon and credit exposure. Credit exposure mean open orders, open delivery and open invoice.

T-code for credit management is FD32

T-code to display Credit Master FD33

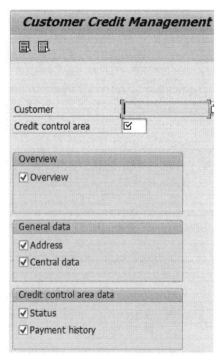

The following are 5 different views of Credit master

- Overview
- Address
- Central Data
- Status
- Payment history

Credit Exposure:

Credit management is the combination of risk category and credit control area of credit master. Credit exposure considers customer's open sales orders, liabilities, delivery, billing, and posting open document's value and adds them all together. The credit exposure is used for credit controls for the transactions to be blocked.

Credit Check:

There are credit checks.

Credit reports and functionalities

Customer Credit Block:

Customer credit block controls and stops the sales and delivery document for further processing. The sales order requires processing of approval to release it from credit block. The credit block can be removed with the work list report and by following T-codes:

- VKM4   Release credit for sales order and Delivery document
- VKM3   Release credit for sales document
- VKM5   Release credit for Delivery Document

    To release credit using T-code VKM4

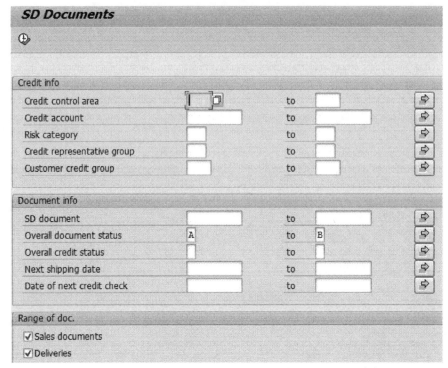

Credit can be released by the report VKM4.

Revenue Account Determination:

Account determination is based on condition technique. Revenue recognition is accounting related functionality. The two types of revenue recognition in systems are:

1. Accrued revenue
2. Deferred revenue

Accrued Revenue:

In Accrued accounting revenue based on recognizing revenue before cash is received. Example even the customer pay for the invoice later, but the review is realized as soon invoice is issued.

Deferred revenue:

Deferred revenue realized later point of time until the amount is received.

Example: when an invoice is created, but the payment is not received, and when payment is received, then revenue is recognized. In other words, the transaction is created, but realization of revenue is not recognized until the payment is cleared then the revenue can be recognized.

Revenue Recognition Configuration:

Revenue recognition, basic and major customization object is Item category. In Item category, we can define what kind of revenue recognition should be applied in the system.

Customization Path from SPRO t-code is the following

IMG →Sales and Distribution → Basic Functions → Account Assignment / Costing → Revenue Recognition → Set Revenue Recognition for Item Categories

Screenshot:

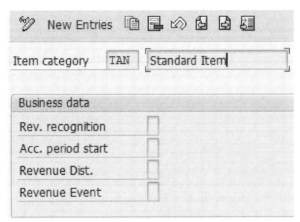

Revenue Recognition field controls if it is standard review recognition, or if it is time related or service related revenue, or Billing related time of service.

Accounting period field if left empty it means it is not relevant for the accounting period start date. This field is for contract and billing related.

Revenue Distribution: This field defines a billing plan related or value with distribution or non-distributions.

Revenue Event: In this field revenue is recognized based on the events are defined in the field. If the event is invoiced or, acceptance date, or it is based on customer types.

Account Determination Configuration:

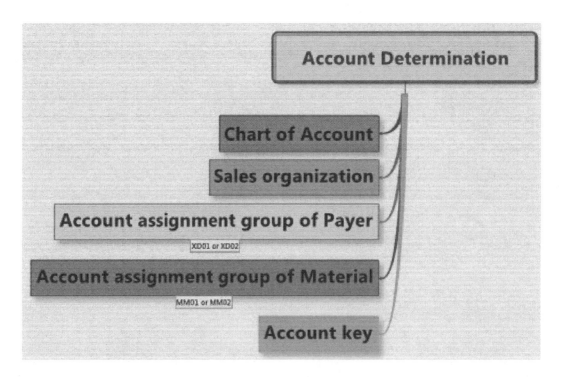

Master Data Account Group:

Revenue account determination is based on customer and material master.

Customization Path from SPRO t-code is the following:

IMG →Sales and Distribution → Basic Functions → Account Assignment / Costing → Revenue

Account Determination → Check Master data relevant for account assignment

In this customization account group gets assigned to customer and material master.

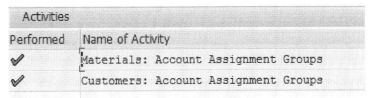

Activities	
Performed	Name of Activity
✓	Materials: Account Assignment Groups
✓	Customers: Account Assignment Groups

Decadency for account Determination:

Dependency for account determination is based on defining the table. The table will be used in the condition technique for account determination. Following standard tables are used in account determination.

Customization Path from SPRO t-code is the following

IMG →Sales and Distribution → Basic Functions → Account Assignment / Costing → Revenue Account Determination → Define Dependencies of Revenue Account Determination

Tab	Short Description
001	Cust.Grp/MaterialGrp/AcctKey
002	Cust.Grp/Account Key
003	Material Grp/Acct Key
004	General
005	Acct Key

Additional table can be maintained for account determination tables.

Define Access Sequence and Account Determinations Type:

In access sequence customization it is assigned to the condition type. Access sequence, then assigns it to the account determination type.

Customization Path from SPRO t-code is the following

IMG →Sales and Distribution → Basic Functions → Account Assignment / Costing → Revenue Account Determination → Define Dependencies of Revenue Account Determination
Screenshot:

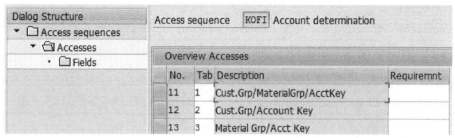

The requirement can be used for system defined options.

Define Condition Type and Assign assess sequence to it

	CTyp	Name	AS	Description
Overview of Condition Types				
	KOFI	Accnt Determination	KOFI	Account determination

In the screenshot above, the standard condition type is assigned to the standard access sequence KOFI. In configuration we will focus on KOFI condition type. In standard system two condition types are used for account determination

- KOFI
- KOFK

KOFI is used for sales from stock where controlling related functionality is not used. The KOFK is used to make to order scenario and controlling is involved like variant configuration made to order and WBS related project system projects.

Define and assign account determination procedure:

In this step we define Account determination procedure controls and assign to the billing document type.

Customization Path from SPRO t-code is the following:

IMG →Sales and Distribution → Basic Functions → Account Assignment / Costing → Revenue Account Determination → Define and assign Account Determination procedure

Screenshot:

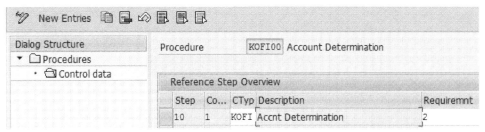

The first field is the procedure and second customization field contain condition type. The requirement type defines if condition type relevant to the controlling assignment of without controlling assignment.

Define and Assign Account Keys

Customization Path from SPRO t-code is the following

IMG →Sales and Distribution → Basic Functions → Account Assignment / Costing → Revenue Account Determination → Define and assign Account Keys

T-CODE: OK11

Screenshot:

In the above screenshot we define an account key.

PR0000 10	0	PR00	Price	ERL	Revenue
20	0	KA00	Sales deal		
40	1	RA00	% Discount from Net		
40	2	RB00	Discount (Value)		

In the above screenshot we assign account keys to the pricing procedure so each condition type of pricing can have different account determination according to the revenue.

Assign G/L Accounts:

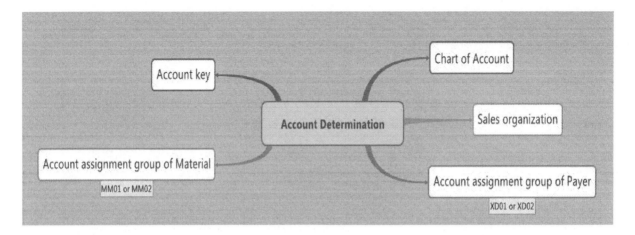

In the last step of account determination G/L account gets assigned to the table conditions are selected in the table.

Customization Path from SPRO t-code is the following:

IMG →Sales and Distribution → Basic Functions → Account Assignment / Costing → Revenue Account Determination → Assign G/L Accounts

T-code: **OK15**

Screenshot:

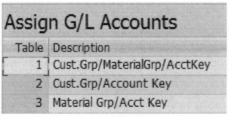

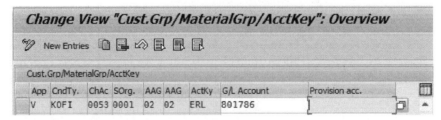

This is general account determination, but it defers based on combinations of Account Key, chart of account, sales organization, account assignment group of customer master, and account assignment group from material master.

App field defines the "V" for sales and distribution related account determination. "CondTy" used for condition Type. "ChAc" field is used for chart of account. Field "SOrg" used in Sales Organization. G/L Account Used for General Ledger Account and Provision Acc. The field is used for accruals for the rebate.

Posting Period:

Posting period is accounting function from monthly statement. It is a monthly period to be open for transactions or closed at the end of the month. A posting period in SAP goes with a month plus years and the status of being open and close for the period.

Chapter 7 Summary

Billing and Credit Management

In Billing following topics are covered in the chapter

- Introduction to Billing
- Billing Order Type Customization
- Billing document type Copy Control
- Invoice List Customization

For Credit management following Topics are covered in the 6th chapter

- Credit Control area customization
- Credit Management
- Credit reports and functionalities

Revenue Recognition

- Accrued Revenue
- Deferred Revenue
- Revenue Determination

Notes

CHAPTER 8

AVAILABLE TO PROMISE

Chapter summary

- Available to Promise (ATP)
- Third party application Interface
- Compliance
- Consignment Process
- Material Determination
- Intro to Resource Related Billing RRB
- Availability to promise and Availability Check
- Output determination

SAP SD Production Order MRP and ATP

History:

Historically ERP systems used to call MRP systems and over time ERP grew out of MRP system and became a small part of the ERP solution.

Business Introduction

Available to promise is based on stocks availability. There are two types of basic processes for allocation process:

- Stock to order
- Make to order

In the stock to order system look at stock and looking at stock could be from purchasing of raw material to production to lead time calculations including in it. Also if we have stock already in plant, then ATP can calculate the shipping time and schedule it accordingly and issue correct ATP date so customer can have exact date. There are two variations in it:

- Backward scheduling
- Forward scheduling

Both backward and forward scheduling can be used with the scope of the check.

Make to Order:

Make to order good example is custom order, when customer need special produced that is more customized with their need.

SAP ATP

ATP stands for, available to promise. When sales orders are created, it runs MRP based on ATP setup. What is MRP? MRP stands for Material Requirement Planning. It is one of the compound parts of the ERP system to process Materials planning according to the requirements.

> **To confirm customer order against scope availability called "Availably to promise"**

Available to Promise and Availability Check:

Available to promise is a function of sales, calculating stock in hands to when it can be shipped to the customer. The system can consider the following elements in ATP check. The screenshots are very descriptive how the system can be configured with these elements for ATP.

Availability check	01	Daily requirements
Checking Rule	01	Checking rule 01

Stocks
- ☑ Include safety stock
- ☑ StockInTransfer
- ☑ Incl.quality insp. stock
- ☑ Incl. blocked stock
- ☑ Incl. restricted-use stock
- ☑ W/o subcontracting

Replenishment lead time
- ☐ Check without RLT

Storage location inspection
- ☐ No stor.loc. inspectn

Missing parts processing
Checking period: GR [ ]

In/outward movements
- X Incl.purchase orders
- ☑ Incl. purch.requisitions
- ☑ Incl. dependent reqs
- ☐ Include reservations
- ☑ Include sales reqmts
- ☑ Include deliveries
- ☑ Incl.ship.notificat.

Incl.depen.reservat.	☐	Do not check
Incl.rel.order reqs	X	Check releases for...
Incl. planned orders	X	Check all planned ...
Incl. production orders	X	Take all productio...

Receipts in past [ ] Include receipts from past and future

The above screenshot explains systematic consideration to calculate and process how ATP should work.
There are five major areas considered:

- Stocks
- Replenishment Lead Time
- Storage Location Inspection
- Missing Parts Processing
- In / outward Movements

For example, if we want to consider stock in the transfer or block stock. These are all situations and business process that need to be streamlined than the configuration part can be done in the system. ATP stands for Available to Promise and it is based on master data and transactional data.

How do master data affect MRP?

Material Master Data has four different views for MRP and they all integrate with all different modules.
To view the MRP views, the user can look into MD04 requirement screen.

What is Requirement Type?

The requirement type function used in form material requirement planning views. In MRP view of material master requirement type can be defined. The transfer of requirement functionality is a prerequisite for carrying out the availability check. Transfer of requirement can be configured without availability check, but the availability check will not work without transfer of requirement.

Transfer of requirement

Material requirement is created with customer requested delivery date and quantity. Transfer of requirement takes the requirement and transfer into Material requirement.
The following are two types of requirement:

1. **Individual**
2. **Collective**

Availability check:

Available to promise date is confirmed by availability check. For transfer of requirements, availability check is a prerequisite. It is on schedule line confirmation, and date confirmation for the delivery date. The scope can be configured to check the following:

Plant Stock/warehouse (Delivering Plant)
(Procurement/Production) Lead times
Plant / warehouse processing time (Pick/ pack, load/Unload, transportation planning time/ Good issue/ receipt time)
Schedule line also determines if AC needs to be activated. When a sales order is created, the schedule line determine new delivery data based on stock level and processing time of product out of the plant.

ATP:

Available to promise functionality based on current stock in hand and also ATP check future purchase order and stock transfer coming in and adding them into ATP logic and also calculate material going out. The options and flexibility of the system allow adopting according to the business needs and turn one and off options in ATP function.

Allocation:

Allocation controls the system with options of available quantity, future available quantity, how much per period can be allocated, allocation based on sales history, allocation based on geographical location, allocation based on limited quantity, and many various options available for customization. Material quantity can be limit for the allocation. Allocation quantity can be based on customer / Region.

The three types of allocations are:

- ATP Quantity base
- Product Allocation
- Planning

AC based on Planning:

It is based on Demand planning generated from SAP APO-DP. These are based on markets not based on customers.

Customization of ATP and AC

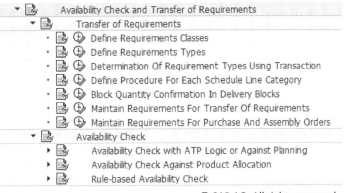

Availability Check and Transfer of Requirements
    Transfer of Requirements
        Define Requirements Classes
        Define Requirements Types
        Determination Of Requirement Types Using Transaction
        Define Procedure For Each Schedule Line Category
        Block Quantity Confirmation In Delivery Blocks
        Maintain Requirements For Transfer Of Requirements
        Maintain Requirements For Purchase And Assembly Orders
    Availability Check
        Availability Check with ATP Logic or Against Planning
            Define Checking Groups
            Define Material Block For Other Users
            Define Checking Groups Default Value
            Carry Out Control For Availability Check
            Define Procedure By Requirements Class
            Define Procedure For Each Schedule Line Category
            Determine Procedure For Each Delivery Item Category
            Checking Rule For Updating Backorders
            Define Default Settings
        Availability Check Against Product Allocation
            Maintain Procedure
            Define Object
            Specify Hierarchy
            Define Consumption Periods
            Control Product Allocation
            Define Flow According To Requirement Category
            Process Flow For Each Schedule Line Category
            Permit Collective Product Allocation In Info Structures
            Check Settings In Product Allocation
        Rule-based Availability Check
            Define business transaction
            Assign business transaction to sales order type

Requirement Class Controls:

1. MRP
2. Requirement consumption strategy
3. Requirement planning strategy

Once ATP and (A.C) availability check are activated, then it is activated globally, but it can be controlled by schedule line to activate or not activated both the functions.

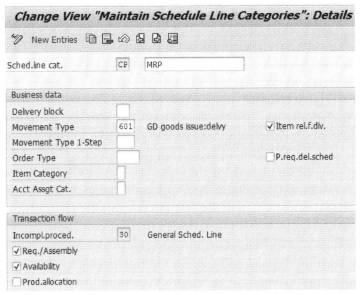

Customization of Requirement Class

from SD prospective the focus on requirement class controls for ATP and AC only; additional customization is out of scope of this book.

In following screenshot requirement class has, availability check and transfer of requirements marked, so these function are active.

In requirement class following elements are controlled:

- Requirments
- Configuration
- Assembly
- Costing
- Account Assignment

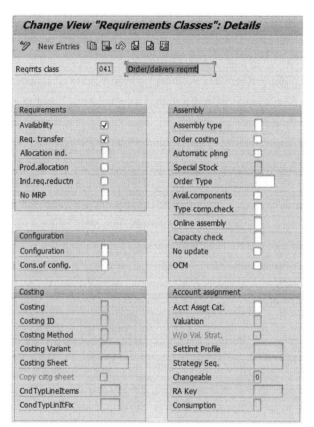

With each customization section it has detail controls for ATP.

Change View "Requirements Classes": Details

New Entries

| Reqmts class | 030 | Sale from stock |

Requirements

Availability	☑
Req. transfer	☑
Allocation ind.	☐
Prod.allocation	☐
Ind.req.reductn	☑
No MRP	1

Assembly

Assembly type	☐
Order costing	☐
Automatic plnng	☐
Special Stock	☐
Order Type	
Avail.components	☐
Type comp.check	☐
Online assembly	☐
Capacity check	☐
No update	☐
OCM	☐

Configuration

Configuration	☐
Cons.of config.	☐

Costing

Costing	☐
Costing ID	☐
Costing Method	☐
Costing Variant	
Costing Sheet	
Copy cstg sheet	☐
CndTypLineItems	
CondTypLinItFix	

Account assignment

Acct Assgt Cat.	☐
Valuation	☐
W/o Val. Strat.	☐
Settlmt Profile	
Strategy Seq.	
Changeable	0
RA Key	
Consumption	☐

Transfer of requirement and availability checked can be controlled from class.

Requirement Type:

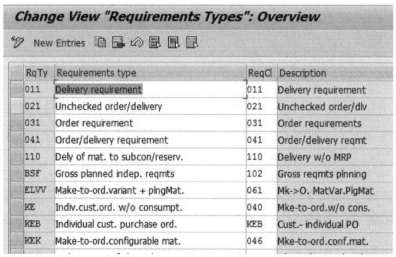

Requirement Type determination

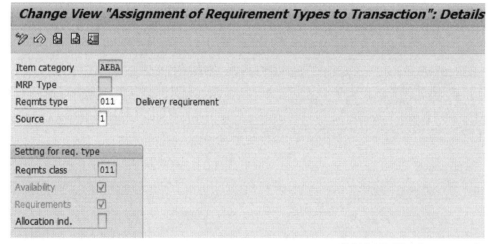

Activate ATP and AC at schedule line category or USE VOV6 same controls

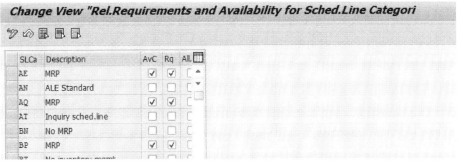

Checking Group:

Checking group controls the AC and ATP further controls.

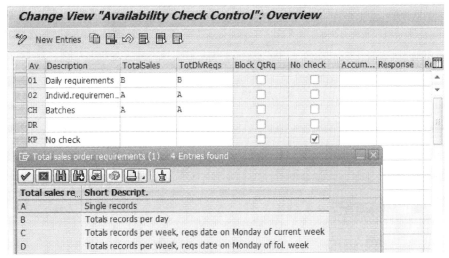

Total Sales requirements:

This configuration is based on sales order requirements and how system controls and should behave for material requirement planning process.

Requirements selections have four options for customizations. These requirements will be generated during sales order creation.

The two different requirements are:

1. Individual requirement
2. Collective requirements

(A) Individual requirement is a single record requirement that is generated requirement for a single item for MRP. The individual requirement processed at a sales level to run MRP and confirm the order and the allocation.

(B) Total records per day is Collective requirement generated based on this option.

(C) It is also collective requirements option. Based on this selection it runs the total requirement based on the week starting from Monday to current week.

(D) It is also similar as option "C", but the exception of it generates requirement for the week, but it generate requirements on following Monday of the current week.

Total Delivery Requirements:

In this configuration, it controls delivery requirement and how the system should calculate it in material requirement planning.

Requirements selections have four options for customization. These requirements will be generated during sales order creation.

Two different requirements are available for selection:

1. Individual requirement
2. Collective requirements

(A) It is in the category of individual requirement, single record requirements generate a requirement for a single item for MRP.

(B) Total records per day is a collective requirement generated based on this option.

(C) It is collective requirements option. Based on this selection it runs the total requirement based on the week starting from Monday to current week.

(D) It is similar as option "C" but the exception of it generates requirement for the week, but it generate requirements on following Monday of the current week.

Block Quantity:

As specified in the settings for quantity block, material will be blocked during the availability check. The quantity reserved for this transaction is recorded in the blocking table. Any other user processing the material at that time received this information. This complements the information gained from the availability check and gives a more accurate picture of the current availability situation. If the block is set, then purchase order, sales order, and master data will be blocked from processing.

No Check:

This customization is configured when availability check is not required for the checking group related controls. If material planning is controlled by third party application or it is maintained out of system, then this functionality is used to turn off the MRP in SAP.

Accumulation:

It customized to avoid inconsistence in confirming quantity of the sales order. Four options available for the configuration of the accumulation calculation. These settings will effect conformation of sales order conform quantity.

1. No Accumulation:

If this is selected in customization, then there will be no accumulation for the sales order. To avoid inconsistency, the alternative option should be used: backorder processing, planning, and rescheduling.

2. Accumulation of confirmed quantity when created and changed:
Based on this customization, the total quantity will be added together on sales order creation. The "accumulation" check ATP quantity and then sales order checked against the available quantity. Confirmation of sales order sum the previous quantity and additional quantity. It basically accumulates the quantity based on customization.

3. Required quantity when created, no accumulation when changed:
It only accumulates quantity only for sales order creation and based on the sales order change, it will not consider ATP quantity.

4. Required quantity when created, conf. Quantity when changed:
It creates a required quantity requirement on sales order creation and based on change, it also confirms the quantity by checking the ATP.

Response:
This function is customized for shortage of material then the system generates an output for the shortage.

RelChkPlan:
This stands for "Relevant check against Planning" and controls for which material should be checked against for planning or plan independent planning.

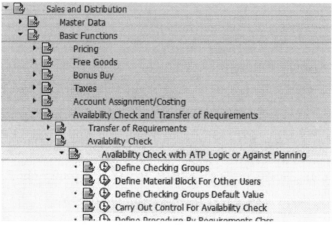

Availability Check Controls:

Availability check can be configured on the following levels of controls:

- Stocks
- Replenishment Lead Time
- Storage location Inspection
- Missing Parts processing
- In/outward Orders Moment

Availability check scope can be customized with many elements to be considered as per the screenshot. As the screenshot represents the following controls:

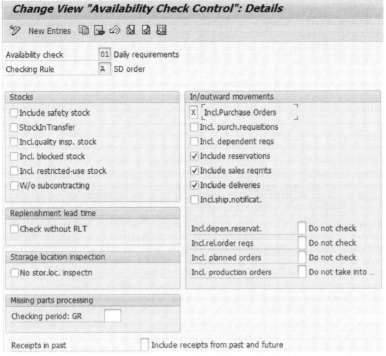

Stocks:

Based on the selection, safety stock can include or exclude in for availability check. If stock is transferred between the plants, system will calculate the time for pick/pack and shipping and loading time. The stock in quality can include or ignore in availability check.

Replenishment Lead Time:

Replenishment Lead Time is based on master data and shipping and loading time, the calculation can be activated for the availability check. The default value can be maintained in the material master.

Extra: Same controls also are used for Total delivery requirements.

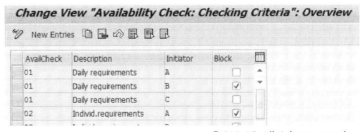

Chapter 8 Summary

In chapter 7 we cover following Topics:

- Material requiring planning
- Available to promise
- Transfer of requirements
- Availability Check
- Allocation
- Availability check based on Planning

Notes

CHAPTER 9

LISTING / EXCLUSION & OUTPUT DETERMINATION

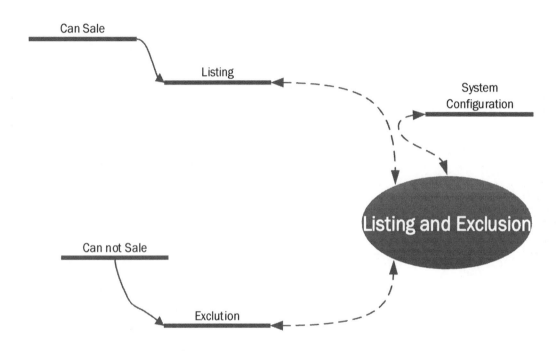

Output Determination:

Output means any type of print form or report that can be printed. In SAP any type of "form" that is created from the transaction can be configured. Output configuration is based on condition technique. Output type can be used for Email, EDI, Fax and other type of interface. The following are few document types where output can be used:

- Inquiry
- Quotation
- Contracts
- Sales related documents
- Delivery
- Billing

The output is not limited to above transactions; it can be used with other transactions.

The output configuration in Sales and Distribution

In Sales and Distribution output configuration customized on following transactions areas:

- Sales activity
- Sales Document
- Billing Document

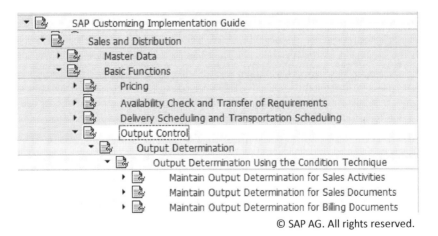

> **Output is form that is printed from transections.**

Output Configuration:

Output determination customization is based on condition technique. The following are customization steps:

- Condition Table
- Access sequence
- Condition Type
- Output procedure
- Condition Record

Output Type Table:

Table customization based on the fields. The fields are the basis of triggering the output type. Also the standard table's entries can be used with access sequence.

Customization Path from SPRO t-code is the following:

IM Customization Path from SPRO t-code is the following:

IMG →Sales and Distribution → Basic Functions → Output Determination → Maintain Output Determination for Sales Document → Maintain Condition Table

T-code for customization: **NACE**

Screenshot:

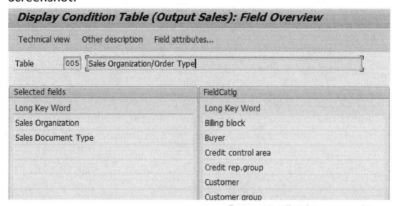

In the screenshot above, the left side display the table field and the right side have field catalog. The field catalog, fields is allowed field that can be used for the condition table.

If the field is not maintained in field catalog, then it's considered an enhancement to add fields in field catalog.

Output Type Access Sequence:

Access sequence is a search criteria, where table entries are maintained. The table eatery can be excluded by customization so the search will stop if the table entry is marked exclusive.

Customization Path from SPRO t-code is the following

IMG →Sales and Distribution → Basic Functions → Output Determination → Maintain Output Determination for Sales Document → Maintain Access Sequence

T-code for customization: **NACE**

In a first step the folder access sequence is selected and new access sequence is created. In the second step the accesses folder is selected with selection of access sequence and table entry can be maintained with requirement and exclusive check box.

Output Condition Type:

Output condition Type is used for the transactional output issue. The output condition type can be manual or can be auto populated with condition record.

Customization Path from SPRO t-code is the following

IMG →Sales and Distribution → Basic Functions → Output Determination → Maintain Output Determination for Sales Document → Maintain Condition Type

Screenshot:

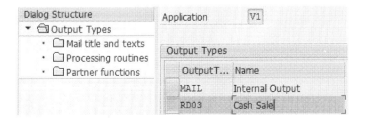

Above is the example of standard output type "RD03" cash sale. The condition type controls are left side of screenshot "Mail title and text", "Processing routine", and "Partner function" has further output condition type controls for customization.

Mail title and text:

Mail title and text used to control the language and document title.

Processing routine:

The layout module controlled that what type of output program is used. There could be multiple processing routine can be used for the single output condition type as per medium. The Processing routine is used to define the program is used in the form and routine is used for the condition type. The customized form is attached to the folder. The PDF/smartform Form is defined in this control and form type.

Partner Function:

Partner function control is used to allow what partner type.

Output type Partner Function Assignment:

Partner functions are maintained with output type for the transaction processing.

Customization Path from SPRO t-code is the following

IMG →Sales and Distribution → Basic Functions → Output Determination → Maintain Output Determination for Sales Document → Assign Output Type to Partner Function

T-code for customization: NACE

Screenshot:

Out.	Med	Funct	Name	Name
RD03	1	SP	Cash Sale	Sold-to Party
RD03	1	BP	Cash Sale	Bill-to Party

Above screen shot defines the kind of medium is used for the partner function.

Output Determination Procedure:

Output determination procedure contains all the condition type for the output process. With output procedure, it is identified with application and usage.

Customization Path from SPRO t-code is the following:

IMG →Sales and Distribution → Basic Functions → Output Determination → Maintain Output Determination for Sales Document → Assign Output Type to Partner Function

T-code for customization: NACE

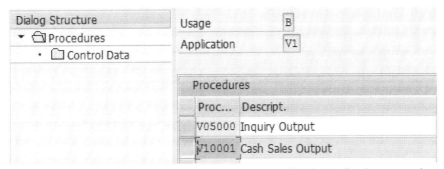

Above screenshot has output procedure type "V10001" for cash ales output type.

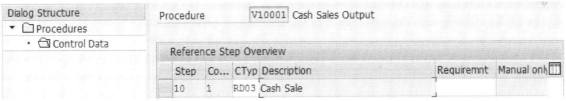

The above screen represents the controls and condition types in the output procedure.

The step field represents the sequential procedure. **Setup** is starting point for processing and **counter** used for same control which sequence the procedure process the **condition type** with the same step. The "**requirement**" is based on what kind of transaction this condition type should be used. Manual only controls if the condition type is manual only.

Output Determination Procedure Assignment:

Output procedure can be assigned on order header and item level.

IMG →Sales and Distribution → Basic Functions → Output Determination → Maintain Output Determination for Sales Document → Assign Output Determination Procedure

T-code for customization: **NACE**

Screenshot:

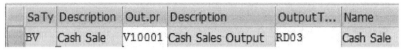

	SaTy	Description	Out.pr	Description	OutputT...	Name
	BV	Cash Sale	V10001	Cash Sales Output	RD03	Cash Sale

Output type and procedure get assigned to the order type.

Item Level Output determination, assignment:

	Item category	Description	Item output proc.	Description
	TAN	Standard Item	V10001	Cash Sales Output

In the above screenshot output determination procedure is assigned to the item category at item level.

Text Determination

Text is used in master data for the transactions and also customized at transactional level too. The text types are used in text determination to be determined for different order type and customer master account group. Document text determination used in header and item level. In text determination, we do not create condition record.

Following steps are used for configuration:

- Define Text Type
- Define Access Sequence
- Define Text Determine Procedure

Define Text Type:

Text type is used in document type and master data. It is define what kind of text it is and assigned to the text procedure.

Customization Path from SPRO t-code is the following:

IMG →Sales and Distribution → Basic Functions → Text Control →Define Text Type

T-code for customization: VOTXN

Screenshot:

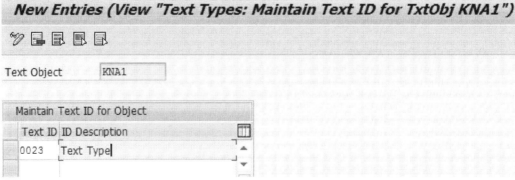

In the above screenshot customization define the text ID type and its description according to the text object.

Define Access Sequence

The access sequence contains the entries for an item and header level text types.

IMG →Sales and Distribution → Basic Functions → Text Control →Define Text Access Sequence

T-code for customization:

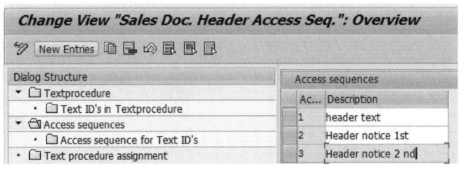

The text access sequence gets assigned to the Text ID type, with additional controls.

Text ID Controls following:

- Text object
- Text ID
- Partner Function
- Take a language from Sales Org
- Language
- Requirement Type
- Data Transfer Routine

Text object could be master data relevant or transactional relevant. Text ID is text type. Partner function defines the partner function Ship to or sold to. The sales organization language took preference for the text. Language can be selected what language is relevant for the text type. Requirement Type is the program that calculates how the text should behave. Requirements are enhancement that can program by the developer. Data transfer is a development object if text needs to be used for selected group of customer or objects.

Define Text Determine Procedure

Text Procedure contains the Text ID types and access sequence controls.

IMG →Sales and Distribution → Basic Functions → Text Control →Define and Assign text determination Procedure

T-code for customization:

Screenshot: **VOTXN**

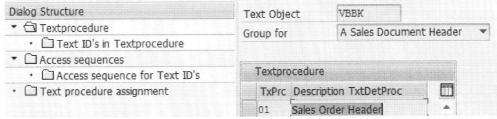

In the above screenshot first we define a procedure with Text object type.

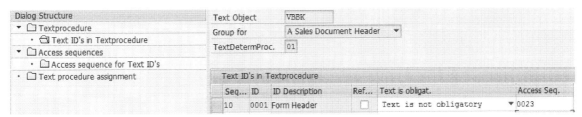

In the above screenshot we define procedure controls with Text ID in Text procedure. The reference field controls if text ID type need to be referenced. The Field "Text is Obligate" controls text to be obligated or not obligate and if it require being display during copying. The access sequence is assigned to the procedure.

Listing / Exclusion

Listing and exclusion functionality define which customer can buy selected product and which product they are not allowed to buy. It is a simple listing concept where material and customer are included. For this we need to group customers and materials and use listing and exclusion.

Listing and Exclusion Customization:

Listing and exclusion is based on condition technique. The customization is maintained under single place where defining table, access sequence, condition type, procedure, and assigning listing and exclusion type to the document type are maintained.

Customization Path from SPRO t-code is the following:

IMG →Sales and Distribution → Basic Functions → Listing and Exclusion → Marinating
Condition Table:

The standard table fulfills most of the requirements.

Listing and Exclusion Access Sequence:

The table is used in access sequence, for the customization.

Customization Path from SPRO t-code is the following:

IMG →Sales and Distribution → Basic Functions → Listing and Exclusion → Marinating Access
Sequence

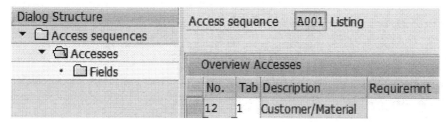

Listing and Exclusion Condition Type:

The condition type has access sequence assigned to it and validity period.

IMG →Sales and Distribution → Basic Functions → Listing and Exclusion → Marinating
Condition Table

	CTyp	Name	AS	Description	Valid from	Valid to
Overview of Condition Types						
	A001	Listing CndTyp	A001	Listing		

Listing and Exclusion Procedure:

Procedure contains condition types with requirement types for the additional requirements in
the procedure.

Customization Path from SPRO is the following:

IMG →Sales and Distribution → Basic Functions → Listing and Exclusion → Marinating Procedure

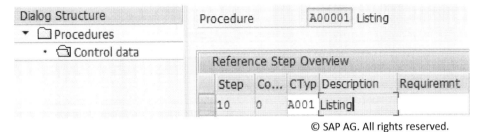

Listing and Exclusion Activate sales document Type:

The listing and exclusion type is assigned to the sales document type. The order type assigned with the listing and exclusion procedure to be determined for the order type.

Customization Path from SPRO t-code is the following:

IMG → Sales and Distribution → Basic Functions → Listing and Exclusion → Activate Listing/Exclusion by sales document Type

	SaTy	Sales Doc. Type	Pro	Listing	Listing	Exclusion	Exclusion
	IN	Inquiry		A00001	Listing	B00001	Exclusion
	QT	Quotation					

> **Listing and Exclusion used for "list" and "exclude" products from sales.**

Chapter 9 Summary

In chapter 9 we cover following Topics:

- Output Determination
- Output determination condition technique
- Output Table customization
- Output Access Sequence customization
- Output condition Type customization
- Output partner function customization
- Output determination
- Output condition Record
- Text Determination
- Listing and Exclusion Customization

Notes

CHAPTER 10

ADVANCED SAP TIPS & TRICKS with VC

SAP Sales and Distribution Determinations:

The following are major determinations of Sales and distribution module determinations.

#	Type	Determination	Comment
1	**Plant Determination**	Customer Material Info Record if exist then Customer Master Record if exist then Material Master Record	System look for first available record
2	**Item Category Determination**	Sales Order Type + Item Category Group + Higher Level Item Category + Usage	item category group come from material master
3	**Schedule line Category Determination**	Item Category + MRP (Materials requirements planning type on the material master record of the item)	
4	**Route Determination**	Departure Zone of Delivering Plant + Shipping Condition of the Sold - to party + Transportation Group + Transportation Zone of the Ship - to party	
5	**Shipping Point Determination**	Shipping Condition of the Sold - to party + Loading Group + Delivering Plant	Loading group come from material Master
6	**Pricing Procedure Determination**	Sales Area + Sales Document Pricing Procedure + Customer Master Record	
7	**Partner Determination**	Sales Document Header/item Customer Master + Delivery Billing Header/ Item	
8	**G/L Account Determination**	Charts of Accounts + Sales Organization + Account assignment group of Payer + Account assignment group for Material + Account Key.	
9	**Warehouse**	Plant + Storage location	
10	**Billing Plan Types Determination**	Sales Document Type + Item Category	
11	**Material Determination**	Sales Document type + Procedure + (condition types + access sequence + condition tables + fields)	
12	**Text Determination Procedure**	Sales Area + Sales Document + Customer Master Record	
13	**Batch Determination**	Material master record	

14	**Staging Area**	Warehouse Number	
15	**Business Area**	Plant + Item Division / Sales Area / Sales Org. + Distribution Channel + Item Division	
16	**Tax Determination**	Taxes according to the Country of the Delivering plant + The Country of the Customer receiving goods + Tax indicator of the Customer master record + Tax indicator of the Material master record	

SAP EDI

SAP EDI stands for the Electronic data interface. EDI is used between two systems to transfer electronic document for business and information exchange. The EDI is standardized by the National Institute of Standards and Technology for organizations. EDI is one of the means for SAP system to another system via EDI, because both SAP and non-SAP can speak EDI language so data transmit. When SAP system talks with non-SAP system, middleware severs will enable for SAP system and non-SAP system to communicate for documents.

IDOC

IDOC stands for intermediate document. IDOC is SAP frame work for interface and it transmits data from EDI interface. IDOC contain data through EDI also middle ware use data packet between systems.

To monitor IDOCS T-code: **WE02**
Test IDOC: **WE19**

How to Monitor IDOCS?

To Monitor IDOC for errors and success following is a screen shot from WE02. IDOCs can be monitors ranged from "Create at" time range. Additional filters can be used to pinpoint the IDOC or periodic monitoring.

IDoc List

Default | Additional | EDI

Created At	00:00:00	to	24:00:00
Created On	11/21/2014	to	11/21/2014
Last Changed at	00:00:00	to	24:00:00
Last Changed on		to	

Direction			
IDoc Number		to	
Current Status		to	

Basic Type		to	
Enhancement		to	
Logical Message		to	
Message Variant		to	
Message Function		to	

Partner Port		to	
Partner Number		to	
Partner Type		to	
Partner Role		to	

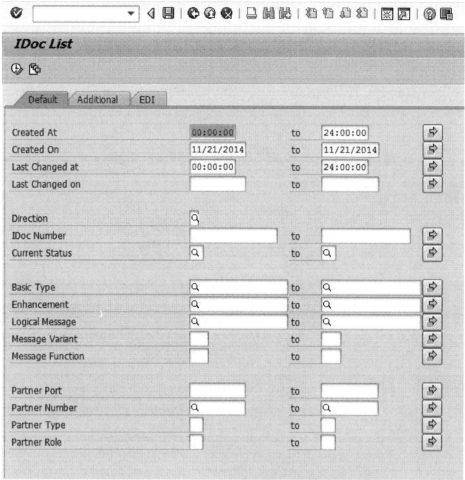

User Exit:

SAP built by ABAP programs is designed and allowed for change called user exit. The user exits are a safe place to be enhanced because they do not affect original functions. These areas are made from modifiable code. The complexity of each business requires their own way of modifying the areas that are different from SAP standard and for editions.

User exit is SAP enhancement areas where programs can be edited and SAP can be molded by the requirement. Each module has their user exits.

BADI:

BADI is SAP related enhancement that functions at the application layer. BADI is a SAP original object that can be enhanced without touching the original object.

Example user can find a BADI and use it to enhance it and original transaction will not be enhanced only the BADI will be enhanced. BADI stands for Business add in. BADI is available to change similar to object oriented programing concept. BADI is used with in bundle of business add-in, Business add-in class and screen enhancement. BADI can use multiple times without touching original object.

BADI is only for application layer changes only. On the creation on BADI the two classes get auto created one for interface and another one for the trigger for the BADI.

To create BADI use t-code SE18

To enhance BADI the user must have developer access to enhanced BADI.

SE19 is used for Enhancement Implementation.

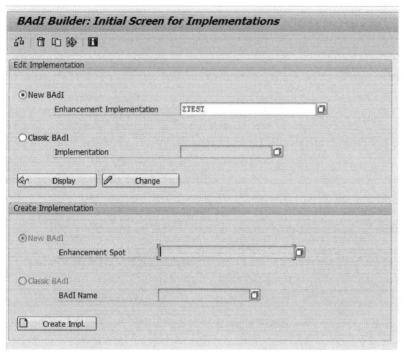

The four sections in this function

Properties
History
Technical
Enchantment Implementation Element

It is more technical in nature, it is technical ABAPER Responsibility.

How to Get BADI?

To search BADI in transaction, the user needs to set bread in class and from the transaction program will stop at BADI.

The steps are:

SE24 and enter Object Type:

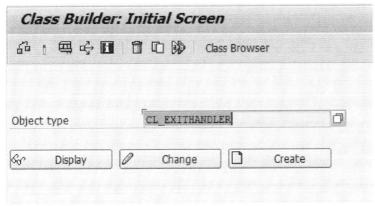

Double click on Get Instance

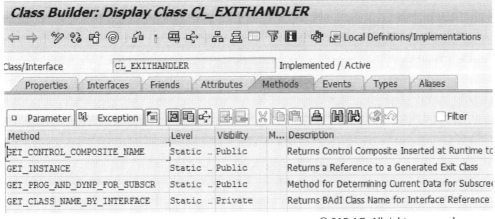

Online no 14 or go to the line which has this value
"CALL METHOD cl_exithandler=>get_class_name_by_interface"

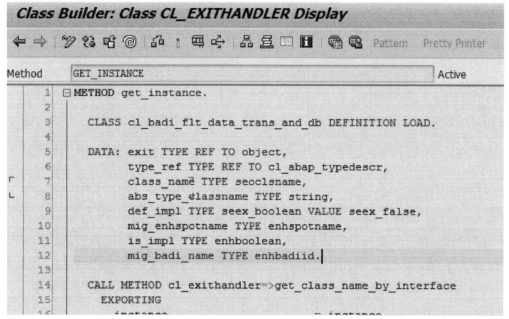

Then select this line and click on 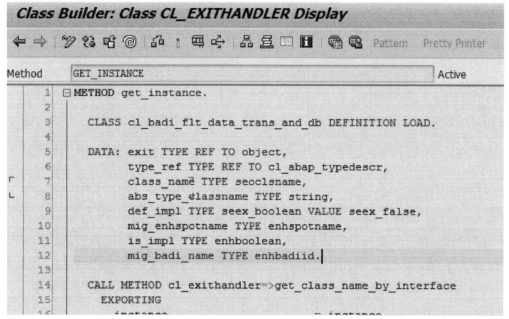 Set/delete session break point or press (Ctrl + Shift + F12)

it should look like that after the breakpoint is set.

After this set in the same session or new session run your transaction to capture BADI

For this example, sales order transaction is used: VA01

The ABAP debugger will pop up and in standard tab and under the local tab on it the EXI name is BADI_SD_SALES is the name of the BADI.

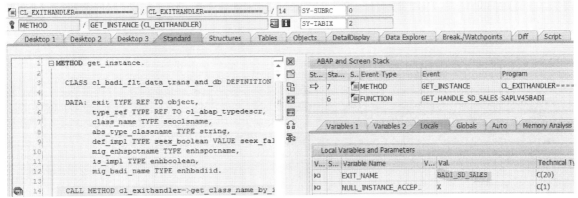

SAP SD Rebate Process and configuration

Rebate process is a kind of discount. In rebate when a customer buys the product they are offering discount on quantity and volume based on date range. The rebate discount is not given to the customer immediately, but the discount is given to customer after a period of time based on the accumulation or periodic basis. The rebate process involves additional conditions and controls that can be utilized in rebate customization. SAP Sales and distribution Rebate process based on rebate agreement. The rebate agreement becomes the basis of accruals on the conditions in the sales process. After the accruals are calculated credit can be issued to the customer. The rebate can be based on customer, material, customer hierarchy, sales volume, and groups. The rebate basis can be changed.

Repeat process can be set for customer for product with a time frame. When the condition of term is meeting then payment will be issued to the customer. In SAP first Rebate agreement is setup based on different criteria and condition master is creating with the time period. Here is a screenshot how rebate agreement looks like.
T-code VB01 to create rebate agreement

Create Material Rebate : Overview Agreement

| [icons] | Conditions | [icons] | Pay | Accrue |

| Agreement | | | Agreement type | 0002 | Material Rebate |

| Description | Material Rebate |

| Extended Bonus | ☐ W/ VAKEY | ☐ Ind. Settlement | ☐ Periodic Settlement |

Rebate Recipient

Rebate recipient	1031	Global Trade AG
Currency	EUR
Payment Method	C	International Check
External description	

Validity

Arrangement calendar	01	Factory calendar Germany standard
Settlement periods	
Validity period	01.01.2013
To	02.01.2013

Control Data

| Agreement Status | | Open |
| Verification levels | F | Display totals by payer/material |

T-Code	Description
VB(1	Rebate number ranges
VB(2	Rebate Agreement Type Maintenance
VB(3	Condition Type Groups Overview
VB(4	Condition Types in Condition Type Groups
VB(5	Assignment Condition -> Condition Type Group
VB(6	Rebate Group Maintenance
VB(7	Rebate Agreement Settlement
VB(8	List Rebate Agreements
VB(9	Maintain Sales Deal Types
VB(A	Promotion Type Maintenance
VB(B	Copying Control Maintenance
VB(C	Maintain Copying Control
VB(D	Rebate Agreement Settlement

LSMW:

LSMW stands for Legacy System Migration Workbench; it is data migration tool comes with SAP 5.0 and 6.0. LSMW transfer data from Legacy system to SAP. It actually takes data from a file and then migrates into SAP. It is used for transfer Master Data and Transnational data before cutover activities. We can use this tool for each object with required fields and additional fields. Most common effective ways is to transfer data into flat files and load into LSMW. In LSMW data can be transferred using existing BAPI, BDC and recording. Flat files mapped to the BDC

(Recording), Program, IDOC and BAPI and loaded into the SAP.

T-code: LSMW

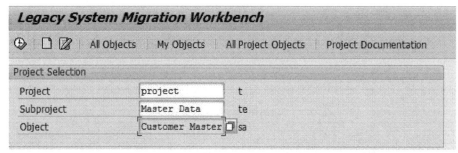

Master and Transactional Data Migration to SAP (add in data migration)

In SAP project implementation, data migration is a critical part of the project. Master Data is the basis of transactional data. After the data extraction from legacy system the data should be ready for further steps. Following is figure of data migration process.

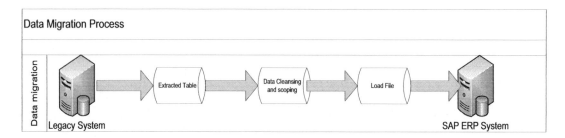

The above diagram is a data migration example, data migration uses many tools and process steps for data migration. After processing steps of: data extraction, data transformation, and load file preparation, mapping the load file is used for final data population. The extracted data could be based many tables. If data is spread across many tables and has multiple record, then it require very careful mapping for comprehensive mapping of valid master data.

Cross matching for Duplicates

Cross matching report identifies duplicate sales order. The duplication of order could be based on many reasons but with this the duplicated order can be cached and fixed.

Benefits:

The crosshatch transaction can help to avoid the error and data duplication. If the sales order is created due to many reasons the order can be identified in this report. The transaction can be run by end user customer service reprehensive or the manager to monitor if duplicated sales order getting generated to avoid duplication.

Transaction code is: **VC15**

Screenshot of **VC15**

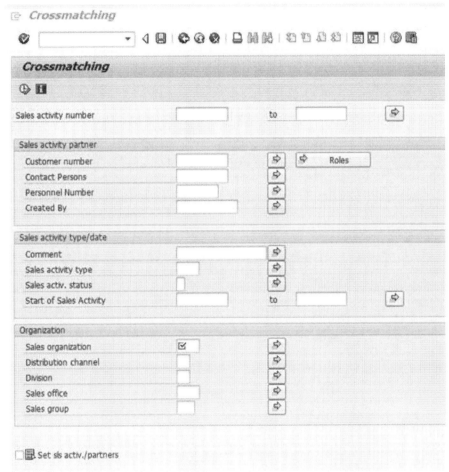

Sales organization filed is required field for the Crosshatching report.

Multiple options available to search the cross match to monitor. The Search can be based on customer number, sales activity or searched by "Created By" user if user wants to validate.

Matrix Copy:

In SAP copy control require an additional shortcut to copy, paste, and this copy paste function in SAP called Matrix Copy.

CTRL + Y Select
CTRL + C
CTRL + V

Reports:

Reports in all modules can be viewed by T-code **SAP1**
Tip: it should be used from easy Access Manu

T-codes for Reports:

Description	T-code
Sales Order Report	VA05
Inquiry Report	VA15
Quotation Report	VA25
Scheduling Agreement Report	VA45
Contract Report	VA45
Customer Sales Summary	VC/2
Price Report	V/LD
Incomplete Order	V.02
Billing Report	VF05
Rebate Report	VB(B

All the T-code in Tables:
To view all the t-codes table use table **TSTCT**

Looking Up T-codes

To find t-codes use the table TSTCT.

The easy trick is that use language: EN

if you are looking for sales related t-code, then uses a text field to search description.

Controls	Description	Example
*	Use it before the word and it will only search word starting from "*".	*sales
*	Use it in the beginning and end: then it will look in all the text and display at-code no matter where is sales values is used beginning, middle or end.	*sales*

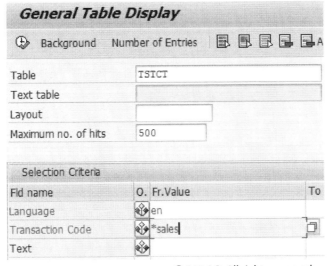

Mass Update:

Following T-codes used for mass update.

Description	T-code
Customer master mass update	XD99
Martial master Mass updates	MM17
Mass Update (many objects)	**MASS**

Mass update Example:

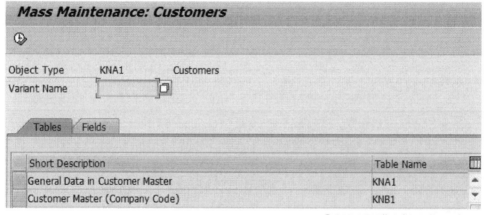

The customer master mass update is based on the tables and field level of customer master. First the table is selected and field is selected and customer range and be selected for the mass update and field values can be updated once.

To view the table:

To view tables in SAP following t-codes are used:

Description	T-code
Table View (Old)	SE16
Table View New	SE16N
ABAP Dictionary	SE11
Run Query	SQVI

Maintaining Pricing:

Pricing tips and tricks for end user

Pricing can be maintained with single T-code: VK32

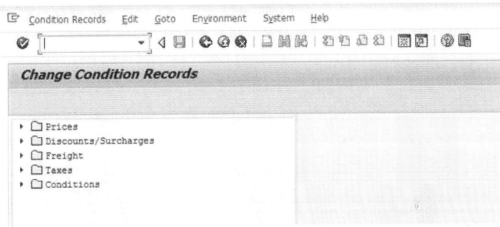

The different type of condition types will be grouped under the respective folder.

Click on the triangle (on the left side of folder icon) and it will drop down the list of condition types under teach folder and user can double click on each one of them to add additional condition records.

Pricing also can be maintained by following T-code:

VK11
VK12
VK13

Create Pricing Record:

VK11 used for pricing condition record from condition type. When condition record is created the respective option on the condition type is setup will prompt for the pricing record. From VK11 user can define scale pricing and condition supplement.

Change Pricing Record:

To change Pricing condition record t-code VK12 is used. It only can be used if pricing condition record exists. With pricing condition record change the record can be marked for delectation.

To view Pricing:

To view pricing condition record VK13 is used for display. With the selected combination multiple records can be displayed in this transaction.

To view pricing report:

This can be viewed from VK32 and also can be displayed from T-code "V/LD" Pricing Report.

SAP official training "Open SAP" and SAP training

Free SAP Training is provided by "Hasso Plattner Institute" with the collaboration of SAP. The training provided to the individuals and student who would like to gain knowledge about SAP.

To gain SAP official training use goes to https://open.sap.com/ and register for current free courses. The courses have opening time and have opening enrolling period. After the enrollment the student will receive an ID and password to start the multimedia course. Their interactive forum for students to contribute toward the class and ask questions on the topic. The course based on video lectures and presentations and it is modular base. At the end of each modular training section it will have a quiz and similarly by the end of course final quiz. The successful candidate will be granted certificate online.

SAP also offers promotional, training official website https://training.sap.com/de/en/. It calls SAP Learning Hub edition, to register for the course please use this code "HUB001". From there users can sign up for a free Couse under the code of HUB001. It is a combination of multiple courses for individuals to learn from. Log in and start learning SAP training today; it has many areas covered from SAP for new student. It also helps who already is SAP end user or consultant to gain knowledge. Please go the website for more details, generally it has basic courses for free, and advance level courses are not free. The course content also limited to the SAP learning Hub edition.

How to register for the SAP Learning Hub edition?

If you are interested in this program, the user requires S-ID.

What is S-ID?

S-ID is used for the training for the prospective student to keep track of his activities. S-ID is a unique ID that is associated with user and need to be requested from SAP training website. First register and request for SAP training ID.

Please send questions and feedback.

BAPI:

BAPI also called functional module that is used for interfaces and programs. BAPI stands for Business Application Programing Interface. BAPI is also called functional module, the BAPI transactions can be viewed with Transaction Code BAPI. BAPI can be called remotely with interface; they can be synchronous or as asynchronous. BAPI used for interface between SAP components to communicate in-between or third party system to communicate with SAP system to process the transaction. To view SAP available BAPI's T-code can be used BAPI.

Following the screenshot of transaction: BAPI

BAPI can be tested with Transaction Code: SE37

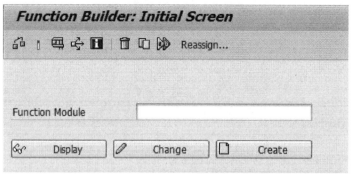

Above screenshot represent the functional module view.

Condition Technique used at following configuration:

- Material Determination
- Pricing (Sales Order, Invoice)
- Text Determination
- Output determination
- Partner determination
- Batch determination
- Free Good
- Rebates
- Revenue account determination
- Listing / exclusion

Third party drop ship

The third party drop ship is based on standard SAP Sales and Distribution functionality.

Business Process:

When a business does not keep a stock of items and have their vendor directly ship their item to the customer it consider drop ship. By drop ship companies save on logistics and have their vendor ship directly to their customer.

Process in Sales and Distribution:

In Sales and Distribution drop ship requires minimal customization. This process involves sales and procurement cycles. From sales side, it involves sales order and billing and from procurement side. It involves purchasing requisition, purchase order, good receipt, and vendor invoice. This process involves order to cash cycle and Procurement to pay cycle.

The following is how it works.

1. Sales order creations
2. Purchase requisition
3. Purchase order
4. Good receipt (Statistical)
5. Vendor Invoice
6. Customer Invoice

Sales Order for Third Party Order:

Sales order flow

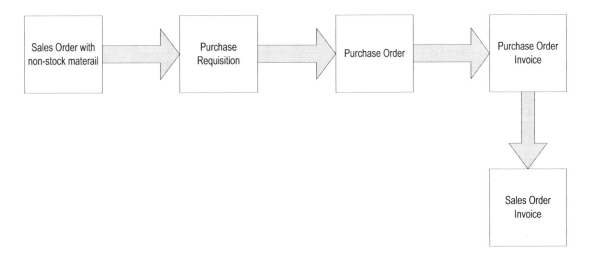

That is a simple third party process where sales invoice is based on sales order related. The sales order has item category "TAS" the item category determine, based on item category group "BARN" from material master. The schedule line has purchase requisition type assigned to it to create purchase requisition. The purchase requisition copy into a purchase order and then based on the Material management, procurement related controls if statically good receipt is required before the vendor invoice or vendor invoice can be created without good receipt. After vendor invoice sales invoice can be created.

Variant:

Variant is shortcut values in SAP transactions. It is used if value needs to be auto populated in transactions, reports and master data processing. The variant icon can be identified with folder.

Variant can be Global or local. The global variant can be seen and used by all the users on the same client. The user variant only can be viewed by the user who created it.

SQVI:

SQVI is table join view t-code. SQVI tool used for database table to connect and create a report. It can create reports from two or more tables together. With this tool reports can be generated with detail customization. SQVI should be used with caution because bad setup of this T-code can affect system performance and hang the database. It is for supper users.

Screenshot:

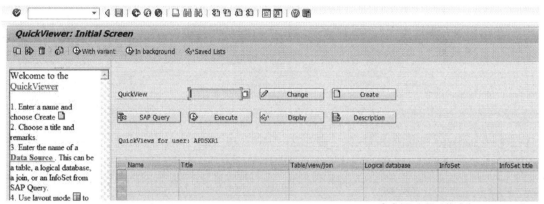

SQVI query could be based on a single table or could be based on the join of tables, or logical database or SAP query infoset. The table and join tale should be sufficient for most of the requirements. The layout of the tables can be select "basic mode" or Layout mode. The layout can be changed even after the tables are selected with filter and selection criteria.

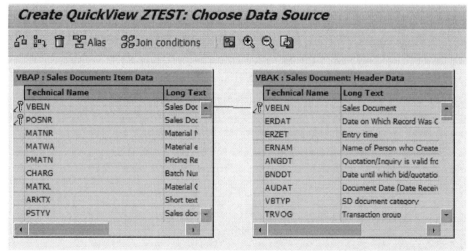

The above screenshot is an example of join tables. The join of table should base on key fields or correct join field, otherwise table entry will not work.

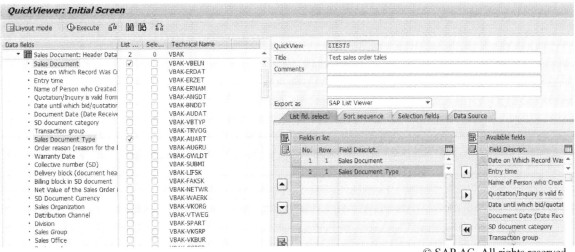

The above screen representing how the report can be selected on the left side of screen fields can be selected and on the right side of screen fields can be selected also and the report then can be executed.

Edit Table Entry:

Table entry should not be updated because it is not recommended by SAP unless the table is custom table, also it can cause an error in the database.

The table can be edited with a few different ways:

- EDIT table from Table View (SE16n)
- Edit Table with ABAP
- Edit Table with SM30
- Maintain Table with SE11

Edit Table With Table View (SE16N):

The table view tool is used for tables display and table data. This transaction does not allow data to be edited in it so it is display only. Data can be edited it from this transaction, but it is not recommended.

Follow the following steps:

1. Go to Table view by entering T-code: SE16N
2. Enter another t-code in the Table view "sap_edit"

3. Execute the table.

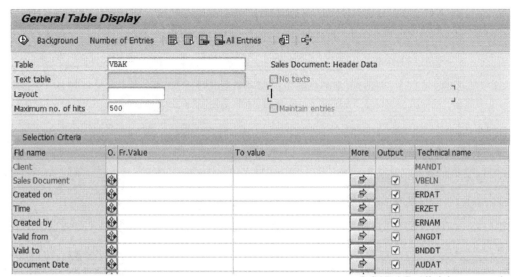

With the "More" button additional values can be searched at once.

SM30 Table Maintenance:

The transaction code is used for table maintenance. With this table customized tables and standard tables can be edited and entries can be added into it.

ABAP and SE11:

SE11 is used by ABAP programmer, here also maintenance of table is possible, and it is more technical compare to functional.

Debugging ABAP program:

Debugging program is used for fixing issues and identifies problems. It can identify what is getting processed by ABAP program. Debugging require ABAP knowledge to understand ABAP program.

Debugging:

To start debugging use the T-code"/h" it will make the debugger on and as soon as transaction or program is started, the system will open a new screen where debugging can be analyzed.

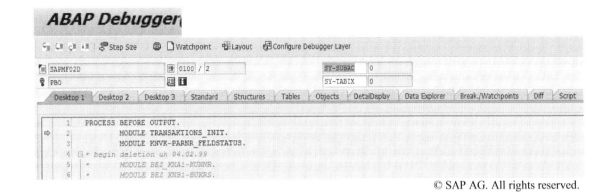

The program has lines with nomadic values where the ABAP debugger can be used for line by line code run or also process all the line and can have stop on certain line value can be viewed.

Tip: To understand ABAP select on Syntax and click on F1 it will show description and maybe an example of the code.

Variant Configuration:

Variant Configuration is SAP term which refers to options in sales order processing with selections. Mostly this function is used in the automotive industry. Variant configuration is a single material that is entered in the sales order and then new screen pop up and user can configure or select options. It also considered as make to order because of selections are unique with a combination of vagrants in the sales process. If we take an example for car sell options, customers can request five CD players instead of a single CD player. There could be many other options available to choose from. The benefit of the options is that material master data maintenance would be only one material with many options or variants. If variant configuration is not used then there would be different materials for each different option and combinations and that can cause data overload and confusions. Variant configuration also reflects its variants in bill of material and pricing. In this book variant configuration setup is based on very basic. Variant configuration involves following modules.

Variant Configuration Sales and Distribution:

Variant configuration related function would be pricing related configuration setup for the material. Variant level pricing different option to option so for this functionality, dependency is

required to be written, and pricing characteristic is also required to be attached to the main class.

Material Master:

The variant configuration material is created with material master type "KMAT". KMAT stands

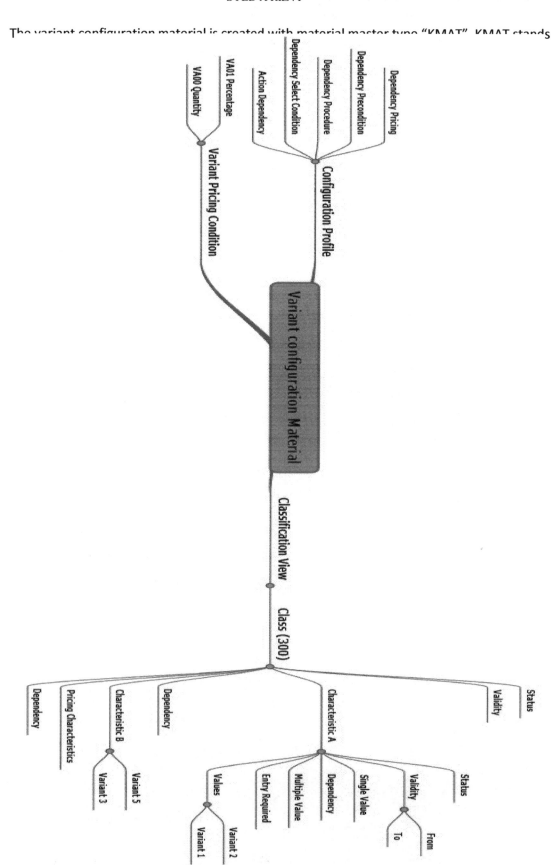

for configurable material. With material type KMAT it comes with configuration preset for variant configurable views and controls for the material.

To create Variant configuration material is: MM01

With Material Master Basic Data 2 the field "Material is Configurable" should be checked.

Also for Classification view should be selected by Class type 300.

The class is required to be created to enter in the material master.

Class:

The class contains many characteristic in it and characteristic has variants in it. Many other types of classes, but Class 300 represents variant class. Variant class 300 allows the function of variant configuration for the material. The class has a validity period. Cass has status, and class can be created specific to organizational area.

To create class T-code is used is "CL01".

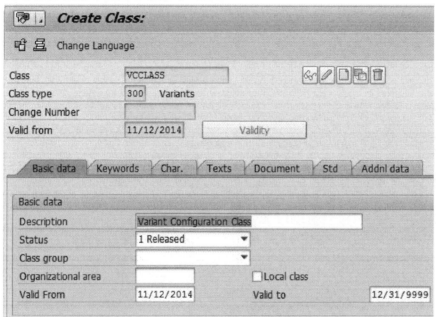

Characteristic are assigned in class in following screenshot

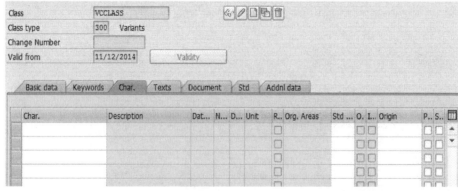

After the class creation characteristic are required to be created to populate in class. Dependency can be written if characteristic is needed to be selected based on a rule. That

means based on the condition or requirement, only few characteristics can be used at the time of sales order creation.

Characteristic

Characteristic contains the variants on it which are selected as an option at the time to make to sales order creation. Characteristic also has validity period and status. Each characteristic has a group of variants grouped in it.

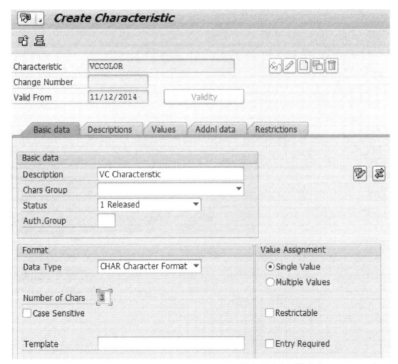

In Basic View, data type should be Character type and length of key which represent variant is selected in basic data.

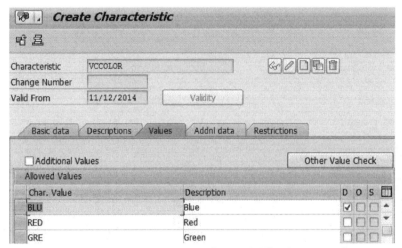

The keys or variants are defined in Values tab.

Pricing Characteristic

Characteristic for pricing is defined without the Values; the pricing Characteristic will be assigned in same class. Base on the pricing Characteristic it will be used for the pricing dependency setup and condition records.

T-code for Characteristic: **CT04**

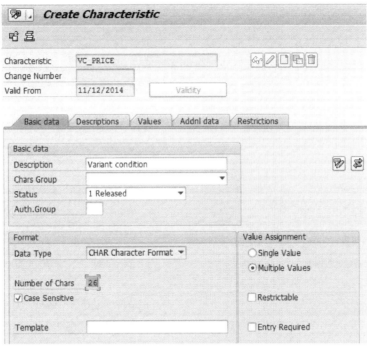

For pricing characteristic value assignment, it needs to be set in multiple Value option and number of char option should be **"26"**.

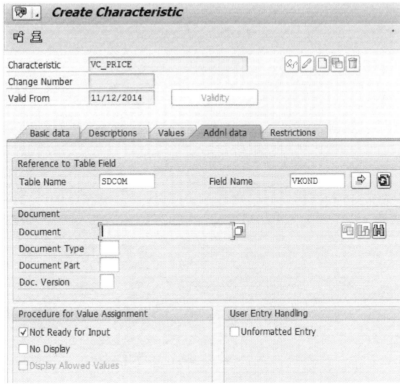

With Additional data view table name need to be populated "SDCOM" and field name "VKNOD". With the table reference multiple variants can be used for pricing. This characteristic does not take direct input so far "procedure for Value Assignment" tab option should be selected "not ready for input".

Variant Configuration, Pricing:

Pricing in variant configuration is part of Sales and Distribution module. Pricing condition type used in variant condition is the following:

- VA00 Condition type used for the fix amount
- VA01 Condition Type used for the percentage

Pricing requires characteristic to be created with table value, none but with the value of tables in additional data tab and maintains tables. Screenshot of characteristic is attached. To create Characteristic use transaction code: CT04

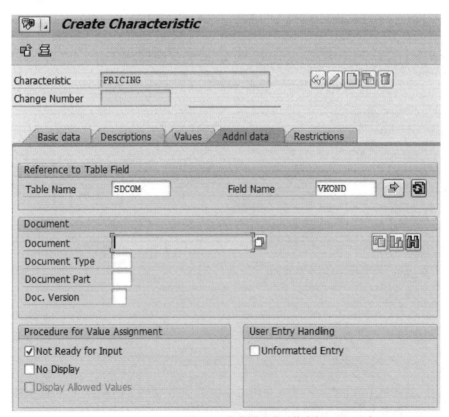

The characteristic is attached to the class that contains variant characteristic. Pricing characteristic is required for pricing to work. Then after the pricing characteristic is maintained, the dependency required to be written for the variant material.

The pricing characteristic gets assigned to the main class where all characteristics are maintained.

Following steps:

The class needs to be assigned into the material master, all the characteristic needs to be assigned to the class. After the assignment of classification and characteristics into material master, the configuration profile needs to be setup.

Configuration Profile:

Configuration Profile is the setup for the martial so the decadency can be assigned to the profile and make bill of material and Sales and Distribution related function possible for the material.

T-code: CU41

Variant Configuration Simulation:

After configuration profile is setup, it needs to be tested. The test can be done for sales configuration, bill of material and plant relevant. Another way to simulate the variant configuration martial is also in the sales order.

T-code: CU50

Dependency:

Dependency is used for condition and calculation controls for the characteristic and class. Dependency can be written in configuration profile, Bill of material items, class, and characteristic. Dependency has two views Basic view and dependency editor. Dependency has four types:

- Precondition
- Action
- Selection Condition

- Procedure

Dependency editor is where the coding is written relates to the dependency. Dependency has following status:

1. Released
2. In preparation
3. Locked

T-code for dependency is: CU01

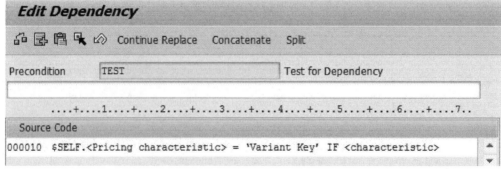

Maintain Dependency: Basic Data

Dependency editor   Descriptions

Dependency   TEST   ☐ SCE Format

General Data

Description   Test for Dependency   ☐ Documentation
Status   2   In preparation
Dependency Group
Maintenance Auth.

Dependency Type
⦿ Precondition   ◯ Action
◯ Selection condition   ◯ Procedure

Dependency for pricing is written in precondition.

Edit Dependency

Continue Replace   Concatenate   Split

Precondition   TEST   Test for Dependency

```
            ....+....1....+....2....+....3....+....4....+....5....+....6....+....7..
Source Code
000010  $SELF.<Pricing characteristic> = 'Variant Key' IF <characteristic>
```

The syntax $SELF is used for characteristic and variant to be defined in dependency.

Syntax: $Self. <Pricing characteristic> = 'Variant Key' IF <characteristic>

= 'characteristic value'

For each additional variant the $SELF statement can be added as follows. Additional controls available for the dependency like, $ROOT and $Parent.

$PARENT & $ROOT:

The statement "$PARENT" used to bill of material related dependency. The parent could be one level above, but it does not mean highest level.
The statement "$ROOT" used for the main item which it refers to the header material.

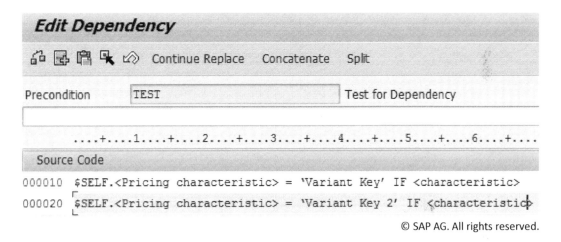

To validate the correct dependency syntax check button (figure Ch 1.1) or shortcut (CTL+F2) can be used to indicate for any errors.

Check Button   **Figure Ch 1.1**

With the help of check the syntax can be fixed and dependency will work accordingly. After the dependency is written and syntax checks the status of dependency need to be updated to "released".

Variant Configuration Trick:

Variant Configuration required many steps like connecting dots between, class, dependency, tabs, characteristics and variant conditions. All the elements of Variant configuration can be managed from single t-code.

T-code: **PMEVC**

From this variant configuration can be done with single t-code. This t-code have many more function that might not be arable from standard variant configuration.

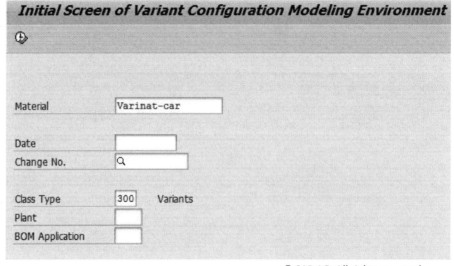

Configuration related Icons

Screenshot	Description	Notes
	Material Configuration	It will open a new screen with item sub item details
	Dependency Object	Dependency can be written in class or characteristic etc.
	Class	Class
	Variant in characteristic	Variant in characteristic
	Bill of Material	BOM
	BOM item	Bill of material item
	Constraint Net	Constraint Net
	Constraint	Constraint
	Procedure	Procedure
	Precondition	Precondition
	Selection Condition	Selection Condition
	Material	Material Master

Parameters and less clicks:

Parameter ID used as user own data, meaning it will be pacific to the user. If user wants to auto populate the data in the processing of transaction, it can help in time and less clicks and keyboard entry for the user. If the same field value is different every time than maintaining the field value to auto populate do not make sense.

Parameter ID can be searched in table TPARA

SAP standard parameter ID sample:

Description	Parameter ID
Parameters for shipping Point	VST
Sold to party in the sales order	VAU
Purchasing Group (MM)	EKO
Currency unit	FWS
Sales organization	VKO
Distribution Channel	VTW

Screenshot: for Parameter maintenance

T-code: **SU3**

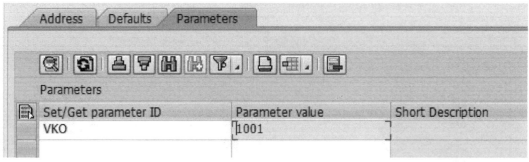

In the above screenshot the parameter ID and parameter value can be managed according to the values are maintained in the system.

For default values for date format, time format, and decimal notation, numbers can also be set from the Defaults Tab.

Address	Defaults	Parameters

Start menu	
Logon Language	
Decimal Notation	K 1,234,567.89 ▼
Date Format	2 MM/DD/YYYY ▼
Time Format (12/24h)	1 12 Hour Format (Example: 12:05:10 PM) ▼

Spool Control

OutputDevice	
☐ Print immed.	
☐ Delete After Output	

Personal Time Zone

Time Zone	

Startup Transaction:

With this setup, the system will start with the transaction automatically every time user log on. To setup the transaction goes to easy access Manu and click on "Extra" and select "Set start Transaction".

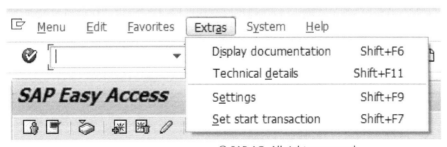

In this transaction code is used for this function.

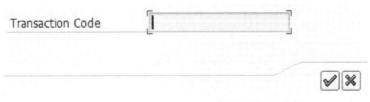

So with that this transaction will be there from a log on the GUI.

SAP ICONS:

Throughout the SAP transactions and configuration, user interact with many icons. How to understand ICON description.

T-code: ICON
With this user can see what this icon means.

Display View "Icon maintenance": Overview

Icon maintenance

+	+	+	+
ICON_PRINT	Print	Print
ICON_CREATE	Create	Create
ICON_CHANGE	Change	Change
ICON_DISPLAY	Display	Display
ICON_DELETE	Delete	Delete
ICON_TEST	Test	Test
ICON_SEARCH	Find	Find
ICON_COPY_OBJECT	Copy <object>	Copy <object>
ICON_EXECUTE_OBJECT	Execute <object>	Execute <object>
ICON_SELECT_DETAIL	Choose <detail>; Detail	Choose <detail>; Detail
ICON_INSERT_ROW	Insert Row	Insert Row
ICON_DELETE_ROW	Delete Row	Delete Row
ICON_MESSAGE_INFORMATION	Information message	Information message
ICON_MESSAGE_WARNING	Warning	Warning
ICON_MESSAGE_ERROR	Error message	Error message
ICON_MESSAGE_QUESTION	Question	Question
ICON_MESSAGE_CRITICAL	Critical message	Critical message
ICON_DISPLAY_MORE	Multiple Selection (Active)	Multiple Selection (Active)
ICON_ENTER_MORE	Multiple selection	Multiple selection
ICON_EQUAL	Equals	Equals
ICON_NOT_EQUAL	Not equal to	Not equal to
ICON_GREATER	Greater than	Greater than
ICON_LESS	Less than	Less than
ICON_GREATER_EQUAL	Greater than or equal to	Greater than or equal to
ICON_LESS_EQUAL	Less than or equal to	Less than or equal to
ICON_INTERVAL_INCLUDE	Include range	Include range
ICON_INTERVAL_EXCLUDE	Exclude range	Exclude range

Click on change pencil icon and user can upload their own icon.

Messages Table:

All the messages are stored in table T100

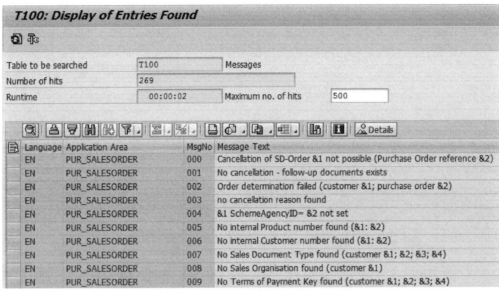

Reports:

Reports can be searched with T-code SAP1. This will update the easy access menu to "SAP Easy Access Report Selection".

T-code: **SAP1**   all the sections will have only reports.

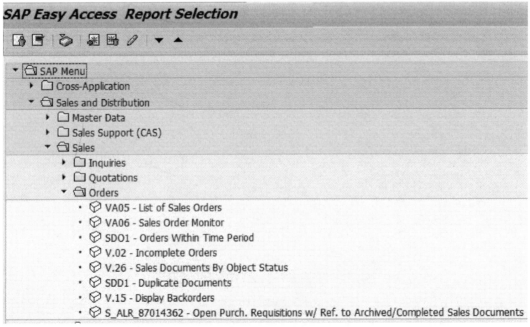

To display additional report use info catalog T-code: SAP2.

T-code: **SAP2**

This transaction displays all the Info catalog reports.

SAP Easy Access Info Catalog

Table View:

The table view function helps understand data stored in the table according to the master data and transactional date or enterprise structure tables.

To View Table following T-codes are used:

- SE16   (Old t-code)
- SE16N   (Upgrade of SE16 and has many options for data mining)
- SE11   (Data Dictionary view, belong to technical views)

Table View Old (SE16)

This is a very basic, yet powerful with full potential use of every function of this table view.

If we use a table it only displays limited fields in the initial screen.

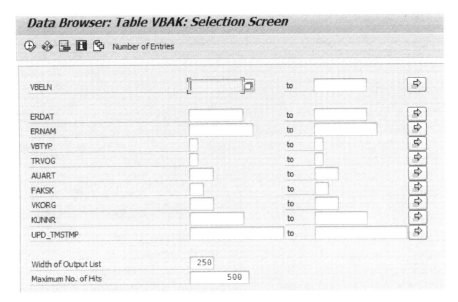

Additional field can be added via Manu option, Setting (Field selected)

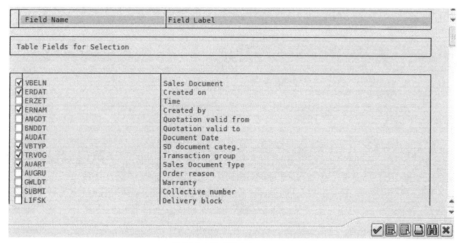

SE16 is old data viewer and can be used, but not allow and show detail information on the first screen and it requires additional steps to use data viewer.

New Table View (SE16N):

The New table view T-code SE16N allow far more functional and contain from the first screen compare to old data view (SE16)

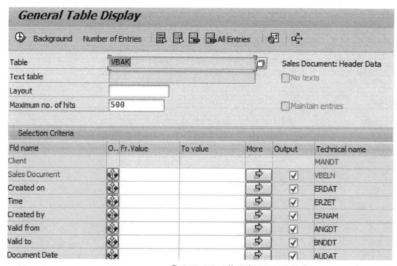

The table view starts with field name which is more understandable compare to technical name of the field.

The table view has option icon which has many controls for the field value to be controlled. Also, it has the same control for more entries to be input in more icons. If output is selected, the table view will show the field results in the table display. The value range can be entered to view according to the range selected from and to.

The Option Icon has many options that can be selected, it will display a dropdown with options.

The More Icon With this multiple entries can be entered in manually or past into it. The more icon can also be used with options for each entry for the controls.

Output

These icon change colors and icon based on selection and entries to reflect status.

Interface:

Third party Application interface:

SAP is leading ERP application software with the capability to integrate with any other application. The sap has flexibility toward third-party application integration with industry standard with standard interfaces. It allows third-party interface connectivity with application component with many technologies. The interface is required to establish for connectivity between applications to transfer or transact. The interface has many connectivity mediums available. The following are a few types available:

- **EDI**
- **BAPI**
- **RFC**

These are few of the many interface technology available by SAP ERP. The interface can be synchronous or as asynchronous and that means that the interface can be real time or based periodically (every hour, daily, weekly, etc.). The interface can also be used for master data or transactional data. Real time interface updates the application in real time as soon as data come in then it gets processed and send back. In asynchronous interface, data doesn't get processed in real time and instead it gets processed in batches or just update the table as per requirement. SAP has EDI capability with IDOC processing with industry standard.

Chapter 10 Summary

In chapter 9 we cover following Topics:

- EDI
- User Exit
- BADI
- Rebate Process
- LSMW
- Cross Match
- BAPI
- Condition Technique
- Third-party Drop ship
- Variant
- SQVI
- Edit Table
- Debugging
- Variant Configuration
- SQVI
- Interface

Notes

About The Author: Syed Awais Rizvi

Syed is senior SAP Sales and Distribution consultant and has worked in numerous implementation projects. He has years of experience in automotive, healthcare, security and various industries. Syed Awais Rizvi serve as the Chief Executive Officer of ITSAS LLC.

SAP Certified Sales and Distribution Consultant.

SAP Certified Project Manager.

IBM Certified System Administrator

ITSAS LLC

Please leave a review on amazon.com

Please leave feedback and comments at rizvir@gmail.com

Subscribe @ http://phtime.com/ for updates!

Thank you

Made in the USA
Lexington, KY
31 July 2015